ALICE
BLOWS A FUSE
Fifty Strip Stories
in American English

JOHN R. BOYD / MARY ANN BOYD

PRENTICE-HALL, INC., Englewood Cliffs, New Jersey 07632

Library of Congress Cataloging in Publication Data

Boyd, John R.
    Alice blows a fuse.

    Includes index.
      1. English language—Text-books for foreigners.
I. Boyd, Mary Ann, joint author.   II. Title.
PE1128.B653   428.6'4   80-10672
ISBN 0-13-022228-3

© 1980 by Prentice-Hall, Inc., Englewood Cliffs, N.J. 07632

Printed in the United States of America

10 9 8 7 6 5

Editorial/production supervision and design by Virginia Rubens
Illustrations by Richard E. Hill
Cover design by Jorge Hernandez
Manufacturing buyer: Harry Baisley

Prentice-Hall International, Inc., London
Prentice-Hall of Australia Pty. Limited, Sydney
Prentice-Hall of Canada, Ltd., Toronto
Prentice-Hall of India Private Limited, New Delhi
Prentice-Hall of Japan, Inc., Tokyo
Prentice-Hall of Southeast Asia Pte. Ltd., Singapore
Whitehall Books Limited, Wellington, New Zealand

Contents

Instructions to the Student

In each unit you will do the following activities:

Part I: Read the sentences in Part I. Be sure you under-stand each sentence. Ask your classmates to explain words you don't understand. Look in your dictionary to find the definitions of unfamiliar words. If necessary, ask your teacher to explain difficult words and phrases.

Part IA: Close your book. Your teacher will give you a strip of paper. This strip of paper will have one of the sentences you just read written on it. Look at the sen-tence and be sure that you know how to pronounce the words. Read the sentence to the class. Ask the class if they can understand the sentence. Repeat your sentence until they all understand.

Listen as your classmates read their sentences. Be sure you understand each sentence. If you don't understand a sen-tence, ask your classmate to read it again. Repeat each sentence after you hear it. After listening to all of the sentences, you and your classmates will then try to choose the first sentence of the story. Listen to their reasons for choosing a sentence--tell if you agree. When you and your classmates all agree, decide on the second sentence. You will continue choosing sentences until you have completed the story. Next, your teacher will tell you to open your book and number the sentences of Part I in the correct story order. Read over the story silently. Be sure that you understand the meaning of the story.

After you have numbered the sentences, your teacher may dictate the story to you sentence by sentence. First the whole sentence will be read. Listen to the sentence while your teacher reads. Then your teacher will read a part of the sentence. Repeat it to yourself and write. Try to write every word. If you don't know a word, leave a space

and continue writing. Your teacher will read the whole sentence again before beginning the next sentence. Check your
work to see if you missed any words. It doesn't matter if
you make a mistake because you will correct your work when
the dictation is finished.

There is one thing you should remember. The purpose of
the dictation is to teach you to listen carefully. Don't ask
your teacher to read slowly or to repeat any words. As you
study this book, your ability to write from dictation will
improve.

Part II: Here's an example of what you will be doing in Part
II. Your teacher will ask you a question about the story.
Then in your book you will put a check next to the right
answer. For example:

Teacher: "Alice is a young woman, isn't she?"

_____ A. No, she isn't.
_____ B. Yes, she is.
_____ C. No, she hasn't.

The questions your teacher asks you will not be difficult.
They are included because they give you practice answering
questions correctly. After all of the questions have been
read, your teacher will ask the questions again and you and
your classmates will answer orally. You can check your
answers and correct any mistakes. Then you will close your
book and your teacher will ask the questions once again.
This time you will answer without looking at your book.

Part III: Your teacher will read you the story you have just
studied. This time it will be in narrative form without
direct reported speech so the verbs will be in the past tense.
After you have heard the story, your teacher will ask you
some questions about the story. Once again you will put
checks next to the correct answers in your book. After you
have put checks next to all of the answers, you will correct
your work. You and your classmates will do this by orally
answering the questions as your teacher reads them to you.
Then you will close your book. When your teacher asks the
questions again, try to answer them without looking at your
book. You do not have to remember the exact words that were
in the answer in your book, but you should try to answer in
an informal manner. This means you don't have to answer in a
complete sentence.

Part IV: The story your teacher read to you in narrative
form is in your book. You will see that every fifth word is
missing. Read the story and fill in each blank. Try to
remember the exact words that were in the story.

Acknowledgments: We would like to offer acknowledgments and
thanks to: John Haskell, Professor of ESL, Northeastern
Illinois University, whose humanistic approach to teaching
has influenced us greatly, and without whom this book would
not have been completed; to Joanna Escobar, Director, Illinois
Statewide ESL/AE Service Center, to whom we are deeply in-
debted for years of guidance and understanding, for all she
has shown us and shared with us; to Richard Schuler, Director,
Illinois State University Laboratory Schools, for starting
the ESL project in the Lab Schools and wholeheartedly sup-
porting us and our efforts there; to Daniel Swanson, Manager,
Bloomington Adult Basic Education, for his sympathetic ear
and patient understanding; to Margaret O'Hara Cain, Nazareth
Academy, who showed us the potential for using the book in
high school remedial English classes; to Pamela Kirshen, ESL
editor at Prentice-Hall, for her encouragement and positive
contributions to the book as it took shape; to our friends
Trong Vu, Mahdieh Araghian, Kathy Lin, Hoan Nguyen and all
of the other students we have worked with during the past
three years--this book was written for them and with their
help.

and to Sarah and Justin, with love.

To the Student: In this book you will be reading about and
talking about stories which tell of the problems of an
American young woman--"Alice Johnson." Alice has many
problems and we hope that the stories about her will start
you talking--first about the story and then about your own
experiences and problems that are like Alice's.

  Alice lives in her own house away from her parents'
home. Her friend--"Mary White"--is in some of the stories.
She is also a young, unmarried working woman living in an
apartment. Another of Alice's friends, a young man named
"Mark Williams," appears in some of the stories. Mark is
not Alice's boyfriend. He is instead like a brother to
Alice--a brother she goes to for advice and friendship.

  Each of the fifty units in the book has a story and
four exercises relating to the story. All of the exercises
in a unit will have the same vocabulary and the same meaning
as the story. We want you to read and listen to the con-
tents of the story each time it is presented to you. With
each exercise you will understand the meaning better.

1

Alice Tries On Shoes

Look over the following sentences and make sure that you understand the words and the meaning of each sentence.

_____ A. "I never can remember. "I'm afraid you'll have to measure my foot," Alice answered.

_____ B. "Well, maybe we should try them in an 8AA," said the salesman, picking up another box.

_____ C. "Yes," replied Alice, "I'd like to try on the pair of tan shoes I saw in your window."

_____ D. "Let me check and see if we have that style in your size," he added.

_____ E. "Oh dear," Alice sighed, "this one's too big."

_1_ F. A salesman came up to Alice as she walked into the shoe store.

_____ G. In a minute he returned from the back room with the shoes Alice had asked for.

_____ H. "I guess you need a 7½AA in this style, ma'am," the salesman said, "and I'm afraid I'm out of that size."

_____ I. "What size do you wear, ma'am?"

_____ J. "Oh, they're too small," Alice said. "They pinch my toes."

_____ K. "Size 7AA," the salesman responded after he had measured Alice's right foot.

_____ L. "Hello," he said, "can I help you?"

3

Part II: Check the appropriate answer to each question
after it is read to you.

1. ___ Yes, she did.   4. ___ Yes, they did.
   ___ Yes, she had.   ___ Yes, they were.
   ___ No, she didn't.   ___ No, they didn't.

2. ___ Yes, she did.   5. ___ Yes, she did.
   ___ Yes, she had.   ___ Yes, she was.
   ___ No, she didn't.   ___ No, she didn't.

3. ___ Yes, he did.
   ___ Yes, he had.
   ___ No, he didn't.

Part III: Listen to the reading passage and then check the
appropriate answer to each question.

1. ___ A. in the store
   ___ B. in the window
   ___ C. in a shoe box

2. ___ A. because the shoes were too big
   ___ B. because the shoes were too small
   ___ C. because she couldn't remember her size

3. ___ A. outside to look at the shoes in the window
   ___ B. in the window to get the shoes she had seen
   ___ C. in the back room to look for the shoes she wanted

4. ___ A. because they were too small
   ___ B. because they were her size
   ___ C. because they were too big

5. ___ A. there weren't any in the style she wanted
   ___ B. there weren't any in the size she needed
   ___ C. there weren't any that didn't pinch her feet

Part IV: Below is the story you just heard. Fill in the
blanks with the appropriate word.

When Alice walked into _____ shoestore a
salesman came _____ to her and asked _____ he could
help her. _____ told him that she _____ seen a
pair of _____ in the window that _____ wanted to
try on. _____, though, he had to _____ her foot,
since Alice _____ remember her size. After _____
her foot, the salesman _____ to the back room to
_____ for a pair of _____ shoes in the style
_____ wanted. In a minute _____ returned and
Alice tried _____ the 7AA shoes. They _____
her feet. The salesman _____ that she try on
_____ 8AA but it was _____ big. A 7½AA
was _____ the size she needed _____ he
was out of _____ size.

5

Alice Is Locked Out

Part I: Look over the following sentences and make sure
          that you understand the words and the meaning of
          each sentence.

_____ A.   "Well, surely you have an extra key somewhere,"
           Mark replied, putting down the mat.

_____ B.   "It's not so dumb, Alice. I've done it myself,"
           Mark assured her as he bent down to look under the
           doormat.

_____ C.   "Well," said Mark, "if it's not in the car maybe
           you left it in the house."

_____ D.   "I can't find my house key," said Alice, looking in
           her purse.

_____ E.   "Oh, I'd never keep an extra under my doormat,"
           Alice said. "That's too dangerous."

_____ F.   "Yes," Alice sighed, "we're locked out. What a dumb
           thing for me to do."

_____ G.   "No, I'm sure I didn't leave it in the car," Alice
           replied.

_____ H.   "I thought maybe you had an extra key under the
           mat," Mark answered.

_____ I.   "You're right, Mark," said Alice. "Now I remember.
           I left it in the house on my dresser."

_____ J.   "What are you doing with my mat?" asked Alice,
           trying not to cry.

_____ K.   "On your dresser!" Mark repeated. "So here we are
           on the front porch, locked out."

_____ L.   "Oh," said Alice, "I just remembered. I gave my
           neighbor my extra key. Our problem is solved."

_____ M.   "Maybe you left it in the car," Mark suggested.

7

Check the appropriate answer to each question after it is read to you.

1. ___ Yes, they were.
   ___ No, they were.
   ___ No, they weren't.

2. ___ Yes, it was.
   ___ No, it wasn't.
   ___ No, it was.

3. ___ No, they weren't.
   ___ No, they were.
   ___ Yes, they were.

4. ___ Yes, he did.
   ___ No, he did.
   ___ No, he didn't.

5. ___ Yes, there was.
   ___ No, there wasn't.
   ___ Yes, there wasn't.

Part III: Listen to the reading passage and then check the appropriate answer to each question.

1. ___ A. in the car
   ___ B. at her neighbors'
   ___ C. inside her purse

2. ___ A. because she had left her key on her dresser
   ___ B. because her key wasn't under the doormat
   ___ C. because her neighbor had her extra key

3. ___ A. in the car
   ___ B. on the dresser
   ___ C. under the doormat

4. ___ A. because her key was on her dresser
   ___ B. because it was too dangerous
   ___ C. because she usually kept her key in her purse

5. ___ A. that her key was on the dresser
   ___ B. that she had given her neighbor her extra key
   ___ C. that she never kept a key under her doormat

Below is the story you just heard. Fill in the
blanks with the appropriate word.

     After looking in her _____, Alice realized that

she _____ find her house key. _____ thought that

it might _____ in the car but _____ was sure she

hadn't _____ it there. When Mark _____ that

maybe Alice had _____ the key inside the _____,

she remembered that her _____ was on her dresser.

_____ Alice realized that she _____ locked out,

she felt _____ had done a dumb _____. Mark

assured her that _____ wasn't dumb as he _____

for another key under _____ doormat. Alice told him

_____ she never kept a _____ under the mat

because _____ was too dangerous. Mark _____

that she must surely _____ an extra key somewhere

_____ then Alice suddenly remembered _____

she had given her _____ a key. Her problem

_____ solved.

9

3

Alice Waits to See Her Doctor

Part I: Look over the following sentences and make sure
          that you understand the words and the meaning of
          each sentence.

_____ A. "Well, Miss Johnson," he said pleasantly, "how's
          your back problem? Does it still bother you to
          sit for long periods of time?"

_____ B. "Miss Johnson," said the nurse, "please come this
          way."

_____ C. "Please have a seat, Miss Johnson," said the
          receptionist. "The doctor's running a little late
          today."

_____ D. Fifteen minutes later the doctor walked into the
          room.

_____ E. As Alice sat down she picked up a magazine and began
          thumbing through the pages.

_____ F. "It'll be a few more minutes," replied the nurse.
          "He's a little behind schedule."

_____ G. "Yes," said Alice, "and at the moment it's killing
          me."

_____ H. "I'm Alice Johnson," she said. "I have an appoint-
          ment for 2:15."

_____ I. "Is the doctor going to see me now?" asked Alice as
          she was shown into a small examining room.

_____ J. Alice walked into the doctor's office and went up
          to the receptionist.

_____ K. Forty-five minutes later she heard the nurse call
          her name.

11

Check the appropriate answer to each question
after it is read to you.

1. ___ Yes, she did.
   ___ No, in fifteen minutes.
   ___ Yes, it was.

4. ___ Yes, she did.
   ___ No, she didn't.
   ___ No, forty-five minutes.

2. ___ Yes, she did.
   ___ No, she talked.
   ___ No, she wasn't.

5. ___ Yes, she did.
   ___ No, she didn't.
   ___ Yes, it did.

3. ___ Yes, he was.
   ___ No, the nurse was.
   ___ No, he wasn't.

Part III: Listen to the reading passage and then check the
appropriate answer to each question.

1. ___ A. because she had to wait forty-five minutes
   ___ B. because the doctor was running late
   ___ C. because she had a back problem

2. ___ A. because her appointment was for 2:15
   ___ B. because the doctor was running late
   ___ C. because she had to wait in the small examining
   room

3. ___ A. she thumbed through a magazine
   ___ B. the doctor saw her
   ___ C. she went into a small examining room and waited
   fifteen more minutes

4. ___ A. if she had been waiting forty-five minutes
   ___ B. how long she had been waiting
   ___ C. if she still had her back problem

5. ___ A. because she had been sitting for an hour
   ___ B. because she was in the small examining room
   ___ C. because the doctor wanted to know about her back
   problem

Part IV: Below is the story you just heard. Fill in the blanks with the appropriate word.

Alice gave her name _____ the receptionist in

the _____ office. She had an _____ for 2:15 but

the _____ told her to have _____ seat because

the doctor _____ running a little late. _____

spent forty-five minutes thumbing _____ a magazine

before the _____ called her name. As _____

was shown into a _____ examining room, Alice asked

_____ the doctor would see _____ then. The

nurse explained _____ the doctor was behind

_____ and she would have _____ wait a few

more _____. When the doctor walked _____ the

room about fifteen _____ later, he asked Alice

_____ her back problem was. _____ wanted

to know if _____ still bothered her to _____

for long periods of _____. Alice said yes, adding

_____ at that moment it _____ killing

her.

4

Alice Has a Problem with her Gas Oven

Part I: Look over the following sentences and make sure that you understand the words and the meaning of each sentence.

_____ A. "I think it's in the back under the oven bottom," Mary said.

_____ B. "Well, how do I light it without blowing myself up?" laughed Alice.

_____ C. "I've got a problem. My oven won't light," answered Alice.

_____ D. "Yoo-hoo, anybody home?" Mary called at Alice's back door.

_____ E. Bending down and removing the oven bottom, Alice asked, "Is that it, there under the oven burner?"

_____ F. "Well, what about the oven pilot light? Did you check that?"

_____ G. "What are you up to?" asked Mary as she walked in and took a seat at Alice's kitchen table.

_____ H. "Yes, and they work fine," Alice responded. "So I know there's nothing wrong with the gas supply."

_____ I. "Just be sure your oven's turned off," answered Mary, "then wait about five minutes before you hold a lighted match to it."

_____ J. "Yes, that's it, Alice. The thing with the tubes leading into it."

_____ K. "Just your oven? What about the burners? Have you tried them?" Mary asked.

_____ L. "I would if I knew where it was," Alice laughed.

_____ M. "Mary, is that you?" Alice called back. "Come on in, I'm in the kitchen."

15

Part II: Check the appropriate answer to each question
           after it is read to you.

1. ___ No, she didn't.   4. ___ Yes, they were.
   ___ No, she wasn't.   ___ Yes, they would.
   ___ Yes, she did.   ___ Yes, they did.

2. ___ Yes, it would.   5. ___ Yes, she did.
   ___ No, it wouldn't.   ___ Yes, she was.
   ___ No, it didn't.   ___ Yes, she should.

3. ___ Yes, they were.
   ___ No, they weren't.
   ___ No, they didn't.

Part III: Listen to the reading passage and then check the
           appropriate answer to each question.

1. ___ A. at the kitchen table
   ___ B. at the back door
   ___ C. in the kitchen

2. ___ A. her burners wouldn't light
   ___ B. something was wrong with the gas supply
   ___ C. her oven wouldn't light

3. ___ A. because the burners worked
   ___ B. because the pilot light worked
   ___ C. because the oven worked

4. ___ A. just the pilot light
   ___ B. just the oven burner
   ___ C. both the pilot light and the oven burner

5. ___ A. that the burners were turned off
   ___ B. that the pilot light was turned off
   ___ C. that the oven was turned off

16

Below is the story you just heard. Fill in the blanks with the appropriate word.

    Alice was in the _____ when her friend Mary

_____ "Yoo-hoo" at the _____ door. When she

entered _____ kitchen, she learned that _____

oven wouldn't light. The _____ were working, so

they _____ that there was nothing _____

with the gas supply. _____ suggested that Alice

check _____ oven pilot but Alice _____ her

laughingly that she _____ know where it was.

_____ Mary told her where _____ look, Alice

removed the _____ bottom and saw the _____

pilot. Alice nervously asked _____ she could light

the _____ without blowing herself up. _____

told her to be _____ the oven was turned _____.

Then Alice had to _____ five minutes before holding

_____ lighted match up to _____ pilot.

5

Alice Mails a Package

Part I: Look over the following sentences and make sure that you understand the words and the meaning of each sentence.

_____ A. "By surface," the clerk answered, "you'd better plan on six to ten weeks."

_____ B. "Oh, and one more thing," Alice added, handing him the check. "I'm moving next week and I'd like to have my mail forwarded."

_____ C. "I want two aero-grams and three books of stamps, and I'd like to send this to Japan," Alice said, handing a small package to the postal clerk.

_____ D. "And how long will the Post Office forward my mail?" Alice asked as she filled out the card.

_____ E. "That depends," replied Alice, "I know surface is cheaper but how long will it take to get there?"

_____ F. "I guess I'll have to give you a check," Alice said. "I didn't bring that much money with me."

_____ G. "You want it to go by air or surface, ma'am?" asked the clerk, putting the package on the scale.

_____ H. "We'll forward your first class mail for a year but we stop forwarding magazines and other printed material after ninety days."

_____ I. "Six to ten weeks," Alice repeated. "That's too long. I guess I'll have to send it airmail."

_____ J. "That'll be $15.94 for everything," he continued, handing Alice the two aero-grams and the stamps.

_____ K. "Well, let's see," the clerk answered, "here's a change of address card you need to fill out."

_____ L. "Airmail it is then," the clerk responded, stamping the package.

19

Check the appropriate answer to each question
after it is read to you.

1. ___ Yes, she did.
   ___ No, by air.
   ___ No, she wasn't.

4. ___ Yes, she had.
   ___ No, she was going to.
   ___ No, she didn't.

2. ___ Yes, it is.
   ___ No, it isn't.
   ___ No, air is.

5. ___ Yes, they are.
   ___ No, printed material is
   ___ No, for ninety days.

3. ___ Yes, she did.
   ___ No, she didn't.
   ___ No, she wasn't.

Part III: Listen to the reading passage and then check the
appropriate answer to each question.

1. ___ A. because it would take six to ten weeks
   ___ B. because it was cheaper
   ___ C. because it was going to Japan

2. ___ A. because she wanted to mail a package to Japan
   ___ B. because she hadn't brought that much money with
          her
   ___ C. because she wanted to have her mail forwarded

3. ___ A. to Japan
   ___ B. for ninety days
   ___ C. to her new address

4. ___ A. the magazines and printed material
   ___ B. some aero-grams
   ___ C. a change of address card

5. ___ A. for ninety days
   ___ B. for one year
   ___ C. for $15.94

Below is the story you just heard. Fill in the
blanks with the appropriate word.

Alice went to the _____ office to buy some

_____ and aero-grams and to _____ a package

to Japan. _____ wanted to send the _____

surface mail because it _____ cheaper but the postal

_____ told her it would _____ six to ten weeks

_____ get to Japan. Six _____ ten weeks was

too _____ for Alice so she _____ she'd have

to send _____ airmail. The clerk _____

Alice that it would _____ $15.94 for the postage,

_____ and aero-grams. Since Alice _____

brought that much money _____ her she had to

_____ him a check. She _____ wanted to

have her _____ forwarded after she moved

_____ the clerk gave her _____ change of

address card _____ fill out. He told _____

that the post office _____ forward her first class

_____ for a year but _____ and other printed

material _____ only be forwarded for _____

days.

CHAPTER
6

Alice Receives a Gift

Part I: Look over the following sentences and make sure
           that you understand the words and the meaning of
           each sentence.

_____ A.   "Oh, Mark, you shouldn't have," Alice replied as
           she pulled off the ribbon.

_____ B.   "You're more than welcome, Alice," Mark smiled.
           "Come on, I've got my tools. Let's put it up."

_____ C.   "Oh, you don't need an outlet," Mark said. "I
           bought you the kind that uses batteries."

_____ D.   "Practical, huh?" Alice repeated, ripping the paper
           off the box. "Well, whatever it is, I'm sure I'll
           like it."

_____ E.   "The best place is probably the hall ceiling near
           your bedroom," Mark suggested.

_____ F.   "Here, Alice, I brought you a little housewarming
           gift," said Mark, handing her a brightly wrapped
           box.

_____ G.   "You know, I just remembered," Alice added, as she
           returned with the ladder, "we can't put it on the
           ceiling. There's no outlet there."

_____ H.   "Why . . . a smoke detector--what a nice idea!
           Thanks a lot, Mark."

_____ I.   "Now, where should I put it?" Alice asked. "I
           don't want the alarm to go off accidentally when I
           burn something on the stove."

_____ J.   "It's nothing special, Alice. Just something
           practical that I think you need."

_____ K.   "The hall ceiling it is," Alice responded. "Wait a
           minute, I'll get the ladder."

23

Check the appropriate answer to each question after it is read to you.

1. ___ Yes, he did.
   ___ No, he didn't.
   ___ Yes, he had.

2. ___ Yes, she did.
   ___ No, she didn't.
   ___ Yes, she had.

3. ___ Yes, she did.
   ___ Yes, she had.
   ___ No, Mark did.

4. ___ Yes, she did.
   ___ No, only the ladder.
   ___ No, Mark did.

5. ___ Yes, it was.
   ___ No, it wasn't.
   ___ No, there wasn't.

<u>Part III</u>:   Listen to the reading passage and then check the appropriate answer to each question.

1. ___ A. a brightly wrapped housewarming gift
   ___ B. a box of ribbon and paper
   ___ C. something practical which he needed

2. ___ A. there wasn't an outlet
   ___ B. it might go off accidentally
   ___ C. Mark suggested the hall

3. ___ A. on the bedroom ceiling near the hall
   ___ B. on the hall ceiling near the stove
   ___ C. on the hall ceiling near the bedroom

4. ___ A. that there was no outlet on the hall ceiling
   ___ B. that the hall ceiling was the best place
   ___ C. that she might burn something on the stove

5. ___ A. the kind that might go off accidentally
   ___ B. the kind that used batteries
   ___ C. the kind that needed an outlet

24

Below is the story you just heard. Fill in the
blanks with the appropriate word.

Mark brought Alice a _____ wrapped housewarming

gift. It _____ something practical which he _____

she needed. Alice was _____ she would like it,

_____ it was. When she _____ off the ribbon

and _____ and opened the box, _____ saw it was a

_____ detector. After she thanked _____ for

the gift he _____ that they put it _____.

Alice didn't want to _____ it up where the _____

might go off accidentally _____ she burned something

on _____ stove. Mark suggested that _____ best

place for it _____ on the hall ceiling _____ her

bedroom. Alice went _____ get a ladder and _____

she returned with it _____ remembered that there was

_____ outlet for the smoke _____ on the

hall ceiling. _____ was no problem because

_____ had bought her the _____ that used

batteries.

25

7

Alice Goes to the Dentist

Part I: Look over the following sentences and make sure
          that you understand the words and the meaning of
          each sentence.

___11___ A.   Alice felt a sharp pain as the dentist injected the
              Novocaine into her gum.

___8___ B.   "I'll be drilling close to the nerve. Are you
              allergic to Novocaine?" the dentist asked.

___5___ C.   "One of the lower left molars, the one next to my
              wisdom tooth," Alice responded.

___12___ D.   "Tell me," the dentist asked after waiting a few
              minutes, "does that side of your mouth feel com-
              pletely numb?"

___9___ E.   "No, I'm not, Doctor, in fact I can't stand to have
              a tooth filled without Novocaine."

___2___ F.   "Hello, Miss Johnson," he said cheerfully. "What
              can I do for you?"

___7___ G.   "Yes, I'm afraid so, Doctor. It's been about a
              month since I lost it."

___1___ H.   The nurse was putting a bib around Alice's neck
              when the dentist walked into the room.

___4___ I.   "Which one is it?" asked the dentist as he looked
              into her mouth.

___6___ J.   "I see," said the dentist. "It looks like you have
              some decay there."

___3___ K.   "I've lost a filling, Doctor," Alice replied,
              opening her mouth.

___13___ L.   "Yes," Alice replied, "I can't feel a thing."

___10___ M.   "Okay then," the dentist continued, picking up a
              syringe, "this may hurt just a little."

27

Part II: Check the appropriate answer to each question
after it is read to you.

1. ___ Yes, she did.
   ___ Yes, she was.
   ___ Yes, she had.

2. ___ Yes, she did.
   ___ Yes, she was.
   ___ Yes, she had.

3. ___ Yes, she did.
   ___ Yes, she was.
   ___ Yes, she had.

4. ___ Yes, she did.
   ___ Yes, she was.
   ___ Yes, she had.

5. ___ Yes, she did.
   ___ Yes, she was.
   ___ Yes, she had.

Part III: Listen to the reading passage and then check
the appropriate answer to each question.

1. ___ A. the dentist
   ___ B. Alice herself
   ___ C. the nurse

2. ___ A. a month before she went to the dentist
   ___ B. a week before she went to the dentist
   ___ C. only a few days before she went to the dentist

3. ___ A. the upper left molar
   ___ B. the lower right molar
   ___ C. the lower left molar

4. ___ A. because he always used Novocaine
   ___ B. because he had to drill close to the nerve
   ___ C. because Alice was allergic to it

5. ___ A. because he wanted her to take off the bib
   ___ B. because she felt a sharp pain
   ___ C. because he wanted her gum to become numb

Part IV: Below is the story you just heard. Fill in the
blanks with the appropriate word.

   The nurse was putting _____ bib around Alice's

neck _____ the dentist walked into _____ room.

In a cheerful _____ he asked what he _____ do for

her. Alice _____ him that the month _____, she

had lost a _____ out of her lower _____ molar.

After looking into _____ open mouth, the dentist

_____ see that there was _____ decay in the tooth

_____ that he would have _____ drill close to the

_____. Alice told him that _____ wasn't

allergic to Novocaine _____ that in fact she

_____ stand to have a _____ filled without

it. When _____ dentist picked up his _____

and injected the Novocaine _____ her gum Alice felt

_____ sharp pain. After _____ few minutes

Alice's gum _____ completely numb and she _____

that she couldn't feel _____ thing.

Alice Goes to a Hardware Store for Bug Spray

Part I: Look over the following sentences and make sure that you understand the words and the meaning of each sentence.

_____ A. "Let's see," said Mary, picking up another can, "this one's supposed to kill crawling insects-- what does yours say?"

_____ B. "Surely it's not that bad," said Mary, following Alice into the store. "You don't have any roaches, do you? I hate roaches."

_____ C. "Why are you pulling in here, Alice?" Mary asked. "I thought you were done shopping."

_____ D. "Wow!" Mary replied. "You don't need bug spray-- you need an exterminator."

_____ E. "Well, these two should do it then," Mary said, starting for the checkout counter.

_____ F. "Bug spray?" Mary repeated. "Are you having trouble with bugs?"

_____ G. "Well, that's the next step," Alice said, picking up a can of bug spray. "If this doesn't work I'm going to see my landlord and demand he call an exterminator."

_____ H. "Am I having trouble with bugs? You name them, I've got them," Alice said, getting out of her car.

_____ I. "Not so fast, Mary. I need something for flying insects too. I've got a wasps' nest in my hall closet."

_____ J. "I just want to run in here to the hardware store and get some bug spray," Alice answered.

_____ K. "Roaches, silverfish, spiders, centipedes--why, I even found some ants in my bedroom today," Alice answered.

_____ L. "This one's especially for ants," Alice replied.

31

Check the appropriate answer to each question
after it is read to you.

1. ___ Yes, she did.   4. ___ Yes, she did.
   ___ No, she didn't.   ___ No, some could fly.
   ___ Yes, she was.   ___ Yes, that's right.

2. ___ Yes, she did.   5. ___ Yes, there were.
   ___ No, in her bedroom.   ___ Yes, for wasps.
   ___ Yes, there were.   ___ No, she didn't.

3. ___ Yes, she did.
   ___ Yes, she was.
   ___ No, she wasn't.

Part III: Listen to the reading passage and then check the
appropriate answer to each question.

1. ___ A. to call an exterminator
   ___ B. to see her landlord
   ___ C. to buy some bug spray

2. ___ A. that Alice was having trouble with bugs
   ___ B. that Alice was going to see her landlord
   ___ C. that Alice had a wasps' nest in her hall closet

3. ___ A. because she was going to the hardware store
   ___ B. because the bug spray didn't work
   ___ C. because Alice had so many kinds of bugs

4. ___ A. go to the hardware store
   ___ B. demand that her landlord call an exterminator
   ___ C. get some spray for flying insects

5. ___ A. because she needed an exterminator
   ___ B. because she had some ants in her bedroom
   ___ C. because she had a wasps' nest in her hall closet

Part IV: Below is the story you just heard.   Fill in the
blanks with the appropriate word.

Alice wanted to run _____ the hardware store

to _____ some bug spray. Mary _____ surprised

to hear that _____ wanted to know if _____ was

having trouble with _____.   As Alice got out

_____ her car she told _____ that she had

every _____ of bug she could _____.   Mary

thought that surely _____ wasn't that bad but

_____ told her she had _____, silverfish,

spiders, and centipedes as _____ as some ants in

_____ bedroom.   When Mary heard _____, she

said Alice needed _____ exterminator.   Alice agreed

that _____ the bug spray didn't _____ she was

going to _____ her landlord and demand _____

he call an exterminator.   _____ the store Mary

found _____ can of spray that _____ supposed

to kill crawling _____ and Alice got one _____

for ants.   She needed _____ for flying insects too

_____ she had a wasps' _____ in her hall

closet.

Alice Makes an Emergency Call to the Doctor

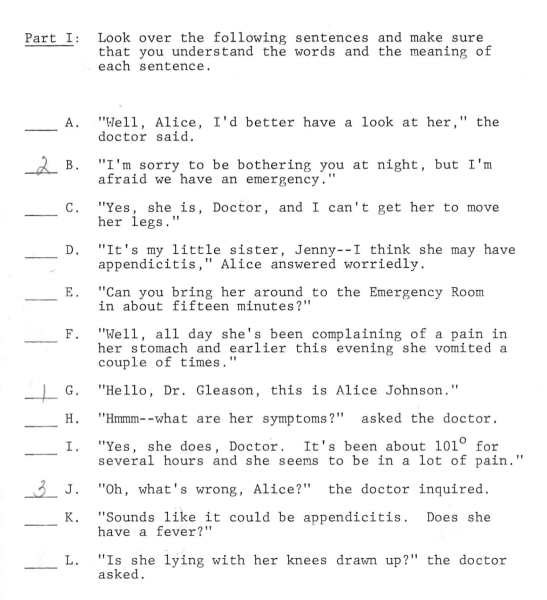

Part I: Look over the following sentences and make sure that you understand the words and the meaning of each sentence.

_____ A. "Well, Alice, I'd better have a look at her," the doctor said.

__2__ B. "I'm sorry to be bothering you at night, but I'm afraid we have an emergency."

_____ C. "Yes, she is, Doctor, and I can't get her to move her legs."

_____ D. "It's my little sister, Jenny--I think she may have appendicitis," Alice answered worriedly.

_____ E. "Can you bring her around to the Emergency Room in about fifteen minutes?"

_____ F. "Well, all day she's been complaining of a pain in her stomach and earlier this evening she vomited a couple of times."

__1__ G. "Hello, Dr. Gleason, this is Alice Johnson."

_____ H. "Hmmm--what are her symptoms?" asked the doctor.

_____ I. "Yes, she does, Doctor. It's been about 101° for several hours and she seems to be in a lot of pain."

__3__ J. "Oh, what's wrong, Alice?" the doctor inquired.

_____ K. "Sounds like it could be appendicitis. Does she have a fever?"

_____ L. "Is she lying with her knees drawn up?" the doctor asked.

35

Part II: Check the appropriate answer to each question
           after it is read to you.

1. ___ Yes, she was.   4. ___ Yes, she had.
   ___ No, she didn't.   ___ No, several times.
   ___ No, her sister was.   ___ Yes, she was.

2. ___ Yes, she did.   5. ___ Yes, he was.
   ___ Yes, she was.   ___ Yes, he had.
   ___ No, she wasn't.   ___ No, Alice was.

3. ___ Yes, she had.
   ___ No, for several hours.
   ___ No, she wasn't.

Part III: Listen to the reading passage and then check the
           appropriate answer to each question.

1. ___ A. she thought her sister might have appendicitis
   ___ B. she didn't know what her sister's symptoms were
   ___ C. she couldn't get her sister to move her legs

2. ___ A. why she was making a late night call
   ___ B. why her sister had her knees drawn up
   ___ C. what her sister's symptoms were

3. ___ A. appendicitis
   ___ B. a pain in her legs
   ___ C. a fever of about 101°

4. ___ A. so he could find out what her symptoms were
   ___ B. so he could examine her
   ___ C. so he could get her to move her legs

5. ___ A. after he heard the symptoms
   ___ B. after he saw her in the Emergency Room
   ___ C. after she had appendicitis

Part IV: Below is the story you just heard. Fill in the
           blanks with the appropriate word.

    Alice thought that her _____ Jenny might have

appendicitis _____ she decided to make _____ late

night phone call _____ her doctor. The doctor

_____ Alice what her sister's _____ were and

Alice replied _____ she had a pain _____ her

stomach. She had _____ vomited a couple of _____

earlier in the evening. _____ was lying with her

_____ drawn up and when _____ had tried to

get _____ to move her legs, _____ wouldn't.

Another symptom was _____ fever of about 101°.

_____ hearing the symptoms, the _____ decided

he had better _____ her and asked Alice _____

bring her sister to _____ hospital Emergency Room.

10

Alice Makes a Flight Reservation

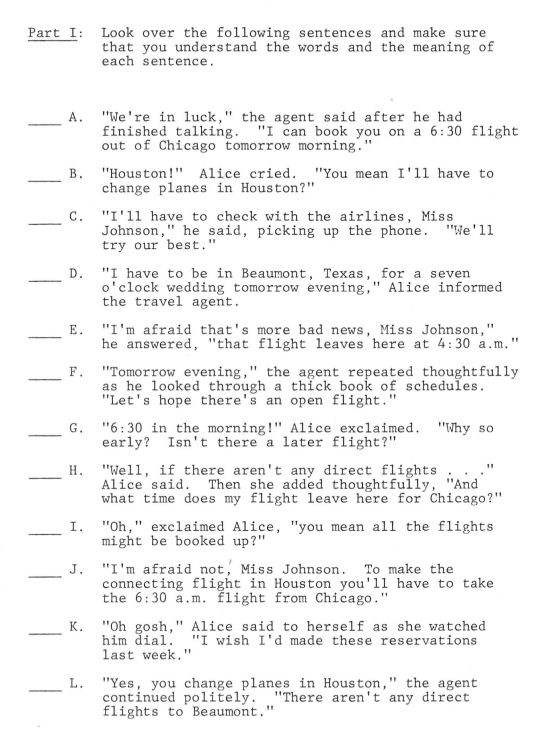

Part I: Look over the following sentences and make sure that you understand the words and the meaning of each sentence.

_____ A.   "We're in luck," the agent said after he had finished talking. "I can book you on a 6:30 flight out of Chicago tomorrow morning."

_____ B.   "Houston!" Alice cried. "You mean I'll have to change planes in Houston?"

_____ C.   "I'll have to check with the airlines, Miss Johnson," he said, picking up the phone. "We'll try our best."

_____ D.   "I have to be in Beaumont, Texas, for a seven o'clock wedding tomorrow evening," Alice informed the travel agent.

_____ E.   "I'm afraid that's more bad news, Miss Johnson," he answered, "that flight leaves here at 4:30 a.m."

_____ F.   "Tomorrow evening," the agent repeated thoughtfully as he looked through a thick book of schedules. "Let's hope there's an open flight."

_____ G.   "6:30 in the morning!" Alice exclaimed. "Why so early? Isn't there a later flight?"

_____ H.   "Well, if there aren't any direct flights . . ." Alice said. Then she added thoughtfully, "And what time does my flight leave here for Chicago?"

_____ I.   "Oh," exclaimed Alice, "you mean all the flights might be booked up?"

_____ J.   "I'm afraid not, Miss Johnson. To make the connecting flight in Houston you'll have to take the 6:30 a.m. flight from Chicago."

_____ K.   "Oh gosh," Alice said to herself as she watched him dial. "I wish I'd made these reservations last week."

_____ L.   "Yes, you change planes in Houston," the agent continued politely. "There aren't any direct flights to Beaumont."

Part II: Check the appropriate answer to each question
            after it is read to you.

1. ___ No, to Houston.   4. ___ Yes, they were.
   ___ No, she didn't.   ___ No, they weren't.
   ___ Yes, she did.   ___ No, there weren't.

2. ___ Yes, she was.   5. ___ Yes, it did.
   ___ No, she wasn't.   ___ No, at 4:30 a.m.
   ___ No, she didn't.   ___ No, it wasn't.

3. ___ No, in Beaumont.
   ___ No, she wasn't.
   ___ Yes, she was.

Part III: Listen to the reading passage and then check the
            appropriate answer to each question.

1. ___ A. she didn't want to go there
   ___ B. to change planes
   ___ C. to attend a wedding

2. ___ A. because all the flights might be booked up
   ___ B. because the agent checked with the airlines
   ___ C. because there was an open flight

3. ___ A. made the flight earlier
   ___ B. made the reservations earlier
   ___ C. checked with the airlines

4. ___ A. in Beaumont
   ___ B. in Beaumont and Houston
   ___ C. in Houston

5. ___ A. because the plane left at 6:30 a.m.
   ___ B. because there were no direct flights
   ___ C. because her plane to Chicago left at 4:30 a.m.

40

Part IV: Below is the story you just heard. Fill in the blanks with the appropriate word.

Alice told the travel _____ she had to be

_____ Beaumont, Texas, to attend _____ wedding

the following evening. _____ agent wasn't sure,

however, _____ there would be an _____ flight

until he had _____ with the airlines. As _____

agent was dialing, Alice _____ to worry and she

_____ that she had made _____ reservations

earlier. Luckily the _____ was able to book _____

on a 6:30 flight _____ of Chicago the next _____.

Alice though wasn't very _____ about getting such an

_____ flight. Then she learned _____ the

agent that there _____ any direct flights to

_____ so she would have _____ change planes in

Houston. _____ he told her the _____ news that

her flight _____ Chicago was going to _____ at

4:30 a.m.

Alice Buys an Ice Cream Cone

Part I: Look over the following sentences and make sure that you understand the words and the meaning of each sentence.

_____ A. "We've got forty-five flavors, ma'am. Just read the sign," she said, pointing to the large board behind her.

_____ B. "Mmmmm, no," Alice sighed, "make it raspberry ripple."

_____ C. "That'll be eighty cents," the girl said, handing the cone to Alice.

_____ D. "A cone," the girl repeated. "What flavor do you want?"

_____ E. "Eighty cents!" Alice exclaimed. "Oh, I didn't bring that much with me. Can you make it one dip?"

_____ F. "Raspberry ripple," repeated the girl, picking up the scoop. "One dip or two?"

_____ G. Alice took a number and waited her turn in the ice cream shop.

_____ H. "Cherry vanilla, strawberry, banana," Alice read. "Gosh, I don't know. I guess I'll take chocolate mint."

_____ I. "What do you want, ma'am?" the tired girl behind the counter asked her when it was finally Alice's turn.

_____ J. "We're out of that, ma'am," the girl replied. "How about peppermint?"

_____ K. Alice thought for a minute. "Two, I guess," she said.

_____ L. "Gee, I don't know. What kinds do you have?" asked Alice.

_____ M. "I'll have a cone," Alice replied.

Check the appropriate answer to each question
after it is read to you.

1. ___ No, she didn't.   4. ___ Yes, it does.
   ___ Yes, she did.   ___ Yes, he does.
   ___ No, she hadn't.   ___ Yes, she does.

2. ___ Yes, they were.   5. ___ No, she didn't.
   ___ Yes, there were.   ___ No, it wasn't.
   ___ No, there weren't.   ___ Yes, she did.

3. ___ No, she wasn't.
   ___ Yes, she was.
   ___ No, it wasn't.

Part III: Listen to the reading passage and then check the
            appropriate answer to each question.

1. ___ A. it would be eighty cents
   ___ B. to read the board
   ___ C. that they were out of chocolate mint

2. ___ A. that was her favorite flavor
   ___ B. they were out of chocolate mint
   ___ C. she didn't bring eighty cents with her

3. ___ A. they were out of that flavor
   ___ B. she wanted raspberry ripple
   ___ C. she didn't know what flavor she wanted

4. ___ A. she didn't have eighty cents
   ___ B. she didn't really like raspberry ripple
   ___ C. she wanted chocolate mint

5. ___ A. more than eighty cents
   ___ B. eighty cents
   ___ C. less than eighty cents

Part IV: Below is the story you just heard. Fill in the blanks with the appropriate word.

Alice took a number _____ waited her turn in

_____ ice cream shop. She _____ she wanted a

cone _____ she didn't know what _____ ice cream

she wanted. _____ she asked the girl _____ the

counter what kinds _____ had, the girl pointed

_____ the sign board behind _____ that listed

forty-five flavors. _____ Alice read the sign,

_____ decided to take chocolate _____.

Unfortunately, they were out _____ that flavor so

the _____ suggested peppermint instead. However,

_____ decided on two dips _____ raspberry

ripple. When the _____ handed Alice the cone,

_____ asked for eighty cents. Alice _____

brought that much money _____ her and she asked

_____ she could change it _____ only one

dip.

12

Alice Blows a Fuse

Part I: Look over the following sentences and make sure
          that you understand the words and the meaning of
          each sentence.

____ A.   "Now you've done it," Mark laughed as the lights
          went out. "You've blown a fuse."

____ B.   "If you've never had to change one," Mark replied,
          "then you probably don't have any extra fuses."

____ C.   "I don't know, Alice," he answered. "Are you
          going to plug it in here in the same outlet?"

____ D.   "Darn!" Alice exclaimed, taking a flashlight out of
          a drawer. "Let's see if we can find the fuse
          box."

____ E.   "Well, if you'll run and get it, I'll try to find
          the fuse box," Mark suggested as he took the flash-
          light out of her hand.

____ F.   "Yes, the same one," Alice answered, picking up the
          iron. "Oh, heck, I think I'll try it."

____ G.   "There you're wrong, Mark. I happen to know I've
          got a fuse in my junk drawer in the kitchen."

____ H.   "You mean you don't know where your fuse box is?"
          Mark asked, following her down the basement stairs.

____ I.   "Mark, will it be okay if I plug in the iron while
          you're using the toaster?" asked Alice.

____ J.   "Just a minute," Alice laughed, taking the flash-
          light back and running upstairs. "You wait here
          in the dark until I get back with the fuse."

____ K.   "Why should I?" Alice answered. "I've never had
          to change a fuse before."

Part II: Check the appropriate answer to each question after it is read to you.

1. ___ Yes, he did.
   ___ No, he didn't.
   ___ Alice did.
   ___ No, she didn't.

2. ___ Yes, she did.
   ___ No, Mark did.
   ___ No, she didn't.

3. ___ Yes, it was.
   ___ Yes, there was.
   ___ No, there wasn't.

4. ___ Yes, he did.
   ___ No, she did.
   ___ No, he never did.

5. ___ Yes, he did.
   ___ No, Alice did.
   ___ No, she didn't.

Part III: Listen to the reading passage and then check the appropriate answer to each question.

1. ___ A. use the toaster
   ___ B. plug in the iron
   ___ C. blow a fuse

2. ___ A. she blew a fuse
   ___ B. she used the toaster
   ___ C. she did some ironing

3. ___ A. to try to find the fuse box
   ___ B. to find a fuse
   ___ C. to plug in the iron

4. ___ A. where the fuses were
   ___ B. where the fuse box was
   ___ C. where the flashlight was

5. ___ A. the fuse box
   ___ B. the outlet
   ___ C. the fuse

Part IV: Below is the story you just heard. Fill in the
blanks with the appropriate word.

Mark was in Alice's _____ using the toaster when

_____ decided to do some _____. She wanted

to plug _____ iron into the same _____ with the

toaster but _____ wasn't sure if it _____ be

okay. Alice, however, _____ to try it, but

_____ she plugged in the _____, she blew a

fuse. _____ a flashlight out of _____ drawer,

she suggested to _____ that they go to _____

basement and try to _____ the fuse box. Mark

_____ surprised that Alice didn't _____ where

her fuse box _____ but Alice answered that _____

had never had to _____ a fuse. She assured

_____ though that she knew she _____ a fuse

in the _____ drawer in her kitchen. _____

wanted her to run _____ get the fuse while _____

took the flashlight and _____ to find the fuse

_____. Alice however, took the _____ back

from Mark and _____ left him to wait _____

the dark while she _____ the fuse.

13

Alice Considers
Buying a Used Car

Part I: Look over the following sentences and make sure
          that you understand the words and the meaning of
          each sentence.

_____ A.   "Well, you might end up with a lemon even if I
            help you. I'm no expert."

_____ B.   "Not a new car," Alice replied, "just a used car.
            I'm afraid I can't afford a new one."

_____ C.   "Well," Alice sighed thoughtfully, "I've got to buy
            a car even if I do get taken."

_____ D.   "I see," said Mark, "you want me to help you. Is
            that it?"

_____ E.   "So you want to buy a new car, Alice," Mark said,
            sipping his coffee.

_____ F.   "But I still can't guarantee you won't get taken,"
            Mark responded. *added*

_____ G.   "A used car," Mark repeated, a little surprised.
            "I guess you know it's risky buying a used one."

_____ H.   "That's right, Mark. I need someone to advise me
            so I won't get a lemon."

_____ I.   "I guess I do know most of the honest dealers,"
            Mark responded.

_____ J.   "Yes, I know it's risky. That's why I invited you
            over," Alice answered with a smile.

_____ K.   "You're more of an expert than I am," Alice laughed,
            "at least you know which car dealers are honest."

Part II: Check the appropriate answer to each question after it is read to you.

1. ___ Yes, she did.
   ___ Yes, she has.
   ___ No, she didn't.

2. ___ No, she couldn't.
   ___ No, she didn't.
   ___ Yes, she could.

3. ___ Yes, she was.
   ___ Yes, she did.
   ___ Yes, she has.

4. ___ No, he isn't.
   ___ Yes, he is.
   ___ Yes, he did.

5. ___ Yes, he could.
   ___ Yes, he would.
   ___ No, he couldn't.

Part III: Listen to the reading passage and then check the appropriate answer to each question.

1. ___ A. a new car
   ___ B. a used car
   ___ C. a lemon

2. ___ A. she didn't want one
   ___ B. she didn't need one
   ___ C. she couldn't afford one

3. ___ A. to help her buy a used car
   ___ B. to talk about lemons
   ___ C. to look at her new car

4. ___ A. Alice did but Mark didn't
   ___ B. both Alice and Mark did
   ___ C. Mark did but Alice didn't

5. ___ A. because all car dealers are honest
   ___ B. because all car dealers try to take people
   ___ C. because some used cars are lemons

Below is the story you just heard. Fill in the
blanks with the appropriate word.

     Alice wanted to buy _____ car. She needed some

_____ so she had invited _____ over. Because

she couldn't _____ a new car, she _____ going

to buy a _____ one and she didn't _____ to get

a lemon. _____ told her that it _____ risky

buying a used _____. She could end up _____ a

lemon even with _____ help. Mark wasn't really

_____ expert but he was _____ of an expert

than _____. At least he knew _____ car

dealers were honest. _____ said, however, that he

_____ guarantee that Alice wouldn't _____

taken. But Alice had _____ buy a car even _____

she did get taken.

14

Alice Cancels a
Doctor's Appointment

Look over the following sentences and make sure
that you understand the words and the meaning of
each sentence.

__7__ A. "Oh, a physical," the receptionist repeated, "and
now you need another appointment."

__10__ B. "Yes, Miss Johnson, physicals take over an hour
and we have to schedule them way in advance."

__4__ C. "I'm sorry, but I won't be able to make it this
afternoon," Alice said. "Something's come up."

__1__ D. "Good morning, Doctors Williams and Brown. May I
help you?" the receptionist asked politely.

__8__ E. "Well," she added, after a pause, "the earliest
Dr. Brown can see you for a physical will be
during the first week of June."

__5__ F. "Well, did you want to make another appointment?"
the receptionist asked.

__11__ G. "Well," said Alice with a sigh, "in that case, I
guess I'd better keep my original appointment."

__3__ H. "That's right, Miss Johnson, we have you down for
3:30," the receptionist responded.

__2__ I. "This is Alice Johnson," answered Alice. "I have an
appointment with Dr. Brown this afternoon."

__9__ J. "June--why, that's over three months away!"
Alice cried, a little shocked.

__12__ K. "Very well, Miss Johnson, I'll put your name back
down and we'll see you today at 3:30," replied the
receptionist.

__6__ L. "Yes, I do, because I've got to have a physical for
my new job," Alice answered.

55

Check the appropriate answer to each question after it is read to you.

1. ___ Yes, she did.
   ___ No, she didn't.
   ___ Yes, it was.

2. ___ Yes, she did.
   ___ No, the receptionist did.
   ___ No, she didn't.

3. ___ Yes, she did.
   ___ Yes, she had.
   ___ No, Alice did.

4. ___ No, the doctor does.
   ___ No, Alice does.
   ___ Yes, they do.

5. ___ Yes, she did.
   ___ No, she didn't.
   ___ No, the receptionist did.

Part III: Listen to the reading passage and then check the appropriate answer to each question.

1. ___ A. because physicals take over an hour
   ___ B. because something had come up
   ___ C. because she needed a physical for her new job

2. ___ A. decided to make another appointment
   ___ B. called the doctor's office
   ___ C. made an appointment for the first week in June

3. ___ A. because June was over three months away
   ___ B. because she wanted to cancel her appointment
   ___ C. because the receptionist said physicals take over an hour

4. ___ A. because Alice canceled her appointment
   ___ B. because the receptionist had to check her book
   ___ C. because they take over an hour

5. ___ A. because the receptionist couldn't give her another appointment
   ___ B. because she couldn't wait three months
   ___ C. because something had come up

Below is the story you just heard. Fill in the blanks with the appropriate word.

Alice called the doctor's _____ to cancel an

appointment _____ had made. She didn't _____

she could make it _____ the 3:30 appointment because

_____ had come up. The _____ canceled her

appointment and _____ Alice if she wanted _____

make another one. Since _____ needed to have a

_____ for her new job, _____ wanted to make

another _____ right away. After checking, _____

receptionist told Alice that _____ could give her

an _____ during the first week _____ June.

Alice was a _____ shocked because June was

_____ three months away. But _____

receptionist explained that physicals _____ over an

hour and _____ to be scheduled way _____

advance. When Alice heard _____ she guessed she

had _____ keep her original appointment, _____

the receptionist told her _____ would see her

at _____.

57

CHAPTER
15

Alice Has Engine Trouble on the Highway

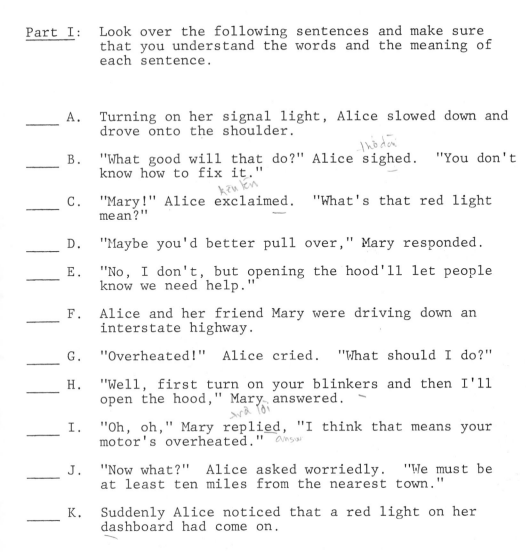

Part I: Look over the following sentences and make sure that you understand the words and the meaning of each sentence.

_____ A. Turning on her signal light, Alice slowed down and drove onto the shoulder.

_____ B. "What good will that do?" Alice sighed. "You don't know how to fix it."

_____ C. "Mary!" Alice exclaimed. "What's that red light mean?"

_____ D. "Maybe you'd better pull over," Mary responded.

_____ E. "No, I don't, but opening the hood'll let people know we need help."

_____ F. Alice and her friend Mary were driving down an interstate highway.

_____ G. "Overheated!" Alice cried. "What should I do?"

_____ H. "Well, first turn on your blinkers and then I'll open the hood," Mary answered.

_____ I. "Oh, oh," Mary replied, "I think that means your motor's overheated."

_____ J. "Now what?" Alice asked worriedly. "We must be at least ten miles from the nearest town."

_____ K. Suddenly Alice noticed that a red light on her dashboard had come on.

Part II: Check the appropriate answer to each question after it is read to you.

1. ___ Yes, she was.
   ___ Yes, she did.
   ___ No, she didn't.

2. ___ Yes, she was.
   ___ Yes, she did.
   ___ No, she didn't.

3. ___ Yes, she was.
   ___ Yes, she did.
   ___ No, she didn't.

4. ___ Yes, she was.
   ___ Yes, she did.
   ___ No, she didn't.

5. ___ Yes, she was.
   ___ Yes, she did.
   ___ No, she didn't.

Part III: Listen to the reading passage and then check the appropriate answer to each question.

1. ___ A. in the motor
   ___ B. under the hood
   ___ C. on the dashboard

2. ___ A. that the motor was overheated
   ___ B. that Alice had to turn on her signal light
   ___ C. that Mary had to open the hood

3. ___ A. because they were ten miles from the nearest town
   ___ B. because the motor was overheated
   ___ C. because Mary didn't know how to fix a car

4. ___ A. open the hood
   ___ B. fix the motor
   ___ C. turn on the signal light

5. ___ A. because the motor was overheated
   ___ B. because it would let people know they needed help
   ___ C. because Alice drove onto the shoulder

60

Part IV: Below is the story you just heard. Fill in the
           blanks with the appropriate word.

While Alice and Mary _were_ driving down an

interstate _highway_, Alice suddenly noticed that

the red light on the _dashboard_ had come on.

Mary _said_ (exclaimed) that the red light _meant_ that

Alice's motor had _overheated_. Alice was upset to

see this and asked Mary _what_ she should

do. Mary _suggested_ (asked) that Alice pull off _the_

highway. After turning on _the_ signal light, Alice

slowed _down_ and drove onto the _shoulder_.

Then Mary told Alice _to_ turn on her blinkers

then she opened the hood. _She_ didn't

think that opening _the_ hood would do any _good_

since Mary didn't know _how_ to fix a car.

Mary replied that although she _didn't_ know

how to fix _a car_, opening the hood would _let_

people know they needed help.

61

Alice Has a Clogged Drain

Part I: Look over the following sentences and make sure
that you understand the words and the meaning of
each sentence.

_____ A. "Yuk! That water looks disgusting," Mary remarked,
looking in the bathtub.

_____ B. "What else can I do?" Alice answered. "I don't
have any drain opener."

_____ C. "And while you're taking your bath," she continued,
"I'll come back here and put some of my drain
opener in your clogged drain."

_____ D. "I know, it makes me sick," Alice replied, "but I
can't get this plunger to work."

_____ E. "Hey, Alice, where are you?" Mary called at Alice's
back door. "It's just about time to go."

_____ F. "I know," said Mary after a moment's thought. "Get
your things and come over and take a bath at my
place."

_____ G. "Well, come in here and you'll see why I'm not
ready," Alice replied, sticking her head out the
bathroom door.

_____ H. "I do," Mary said. "I'll run and get it while you
get ready."

_____ I. "I thought you'd be ready by now," Mary said as she
reached the top of the stairs.

_____ J. "I wouldn't use a plunger on a clogged drain," Mary
advised. "It's too messy."

_____ K. "See," Alice continued as Mary walked in, "I can't
get ready until I get this clogged drain fixed."

_____ L. "But I can't get ready, Mary," Alice replied,
"until I can take a bath. I feel so hot and dirty."

_____ M. "I'm up here in the bathroom, Mary," Alice called
down. "Come on up."

Part II: Check the appropriate answer to each question
after it is read to you.

1. ___ Yes, she was.   4. ___ Yes, she could.
   ___ No, she wasn't.   ___ Yes, she did.
   ___ Yes, she did.   ___ No, she couldn't.

2. ___ Yes, she was.   5. ___ Yes, she was.
   ___ Yes, it was.   ___ No, Mary was.
   ___ Yes, there was.   ___ No, she didn't.

3. ___ No, drain opener.
   ___ No, she wasn't.
   ___ Yes, she was.

Part III: Listen to the reading passage and then check the
appropriate answer to each question.

1. ___ A. because she couldn't get her clogged drain fixed
   ___ B. because it was just about time for them to go
   ___ C. because the plunger was too messy

2. ___ A. she didn't have any drain opener
   ___ B. Mary had some drain opener
   ___ C. the plunger was messy

3. ___ A. the messy plunger
   ___ B. the water in the tub
   ___ C. the clogged drain

4. ___ A. out of the bathroom
   ___ B. over to her place
   ___ C. upstairs to Alice's bathroom

5. ___ A. take her things over
   ___ B. run and get her drain opener
   ___ C. put some of her drain opener in Alice's clogged
          drain

Part IV: Below is the story you just heard.   Fill in the
           blanks with the appropriate word.

     Alice was upstairs in _____ bathroom when Mary

called _____ her.   It was just _____ time

for them to _____ but Alice wasn't ready _____

she couldn't get her _____ bathtub drain fixed.

Both _____ them agreed that the _____ looked

disgusting but Alice _____ have any drain opener

_____ she couldn't get the _____ to work on

the _____.   Mary told Alice that _____ a

plunger was too _____ so she would run _____

get some of her _____ opener while Alice got

_____.   But since Alice couldn't _____ ready

until she'd had _____ bath, Mary suggested that

_____ take her things over _____ Mary's

place and take _____ bath there while she

_____ some of her drain _____ in Alice's

clogged drain.

Alice Calls a Repairman

Part I: Look over the following sentences and make sure
          that you understand the words and the meaning of
          each sentence.

_____ A. "Oh gosh," Alice sighed, "if I have to wait much
          longer my whole basement will be flooded. What
          am I going to do?"

_____ B. "Thank you for waiting," the woman said, coming
          back on the line after a few minutes. "Now what
          can I do for you?"

_____ C. "Oh, I'm glad I got you," Alice said. "I'm Alice
          Johnson and I'm having a problem with . . ."

_____ D. "You're right. That would be dangerous," the woman
          responded. "Well, let me see. What about turning
          off the water?"

_____ E. "I hope I don't get a busy signal," Alice said to
          herself as she dialed the phone. "I've just got to
          get a repairman over here."

_____ F. "I've got a really serious problem," Alice answered.
          "You see, my washing machine's stuck on the fill
          cycle and right now the water's overflowing onto
          the basement floor."

_____ G. "Turning off the water," Alice repeated. "That's a
          great idea. Why didn't I think of that?"

_____ H. "There must be some way you can stop that," the
          woman answered. "Have you thought about unplugging
          it?"

_____ I. "Good afternoon. Thank you for calling Double A
          Appliance Repair," a woman's voice on the telephone
          said.

_____ J. "You do have a problem," the woman responded. "But
          I'm afraid we won't be able to send anybody over
          right away."

_____ K. "I thought of that," Alice replied, "but I'm afraid
          to touch the plug while I'm standing in water."

_____ L. "I wonder how long this'll take," Alice muttered as
          she dragged a chair over to the phone.

_____ M. "Excuse me, ma'am," the voice interrupted, "but I'll
          have to put you on hold. I'm on another line."

67

Part II: Check the appropriate answer to each question
          after it is read to you.

1. ___ Yes, she did.   4. ___ Yes, she had.
   ___ Yes, it was.   ___ No, it wasn't.
   ___ No, she didn't.   ___ No, she hadn't.

2. ___ Yes, she was.   5. ___ Yes, it would have been.
   ___ No, it wasn't.   ___ No, it wouldn't have
   ___ No, for a few   been.
       minutes.   ___ No, she wouldn't have
                                     been.

3. ___ Yes, it was.
   ___ Yes, she was.
   ___ Yes, it did.

Part III: Listen to the reading passage and then check the
           appropriate answer to each question.

1. ___ A. because the woman was on another line
   ___ B. because she didn't get a busy signal
   ___ C. because she needed a repairman

2. ___ A. Alice had to wait on hold for a few minutes
   ___ B. her washing machine was stuck on the fill cycle
   ___ C. the repairman couldn't come right away

3. ___ A. standing in water while unplugging the machine
   ___ B. turning off the water while unplugging the machine
   ___ C. having her washing machine stuck on the fill cycle

4. ___ A. turning off the machine and standing in water
   ___ B. unplugging the machine and turning off the water
   ___ C. turning off the water while unplugging the machine

5. ___ A. unplugging the machine
   ___ B. turning off the machine
   ___ C. turning off the water

68

Part IV: Below is the story you just heard. Fill in the
          blanks with the appropriate word.

        Alice needed a repairman _____ she called the

Double _____ Appliance Repair. She didn't _____

a busy signal but _____ woman who answered was

_____ another line so she _____ to put

Alice on _____ . Alice dragged a chair _____

to the phone and _____ for a few minutes _____

the woman came back _____ the line and asked

_____ Alice wanted. Alice had _____ really

serious problem with _____ washing machine. It

was _____ on the fill cycle _____ the

water was overflowing _____ her basement floor.

The _____ agreed that that was _____ a

problem but said _____ they wouldn't be able

_____ send anybody over right _____ .

For the moment she _____ that Alice unplug the

_____ . Alice had thought of _____ but she

was afraid _____ touch the plug while _____

in water. The _____ agreed that that would _____

dangerous but then asked _____ if she couldn't turn

_____ the water. Alice thought _____ was a

great idea _____ wondered why she hadn't _____

of it herself.

Alice Returns a Blouse

Part I: Look over the following sentences and make sure that you understand the words and the meaning of each sentence.

_____ A. "Oh good," sighed Alice. "I was afraid you might not take it back without a receipt."

_____ B. "Was there anything wrong with it?" asked the salesgirl.

_____ C. "I'm not sure," said Alice. "Does this one come in beige?"

_____ D. Alice stood waiting near the cash register in the women's wear department.

_____ E. "In that case, I'll take a refund," Alice answered. "I don't have to have the receipt, do I?"

_____ F. "Can I help you?" she asked pleasantly.

_____ G. "No, ma'am, since it was a gift it's not necessary," replied the girl.

_____ H. "No, it's just fine," replied Alice, "but it was a gift and I don't like the color."

_____ I. "We don't always," replied the girl, "but I recognized the tag on this blouse."

_____ J. "Let me see," said the girl, taking the blouse and looking at the tag. "No, I'm afraid it doesn't."

_____ K. "Yes," said Alice, handing her a box, "I'd like to return this blouse."

_____ L. When the salesgirl had finished waiting on another customer she turned to Alice.

_____ M. "I see," said the girl. "Do you want an exchange or a refund?"

Check the appropriate answer to each question
after it is read to you.

1. ___ Yes, she was.
   ___ Yes, she did.
   ___ No, she wasn't.

2. ___ Yes, she was.
   ___ Yes, she did.
   ___ No, she wasn't.

3. ___ No, it wasn't.
   ___ Yes, it was.
   ___ No, it didn't.

4. ___ Yes, she did.
   ___ Yes, it was.
   ___ No, she didn't.

5. ___ No, she wasn't.
   ___ No, she didn't.
   ___ Yes, she did.

Part III: Listen to the reading passage and then check the
            appropriate answer to each question.

1. ___ A. near the women's wear department
   ___ B. near the blouses in the women's wear department
   ___ C. near the cash register in the women's wear
          department

2. ___ A. she turned away from Alice
   ___ B. she waited on Alice
   ___ C. she gave Alice a box

3. ___ A. there was something wrong with it
   ___ B. it wasn't the right color
   ___ C. it wasn't the right size

4. ___ A. she wanted the money
   ___ B. she wanted another gift
   ___ C. it didn't come in beige

5. ___ A. because the girl recognized the tag
   ___ B. because she wanted a refund
   ___ C. because she didn't want to exchange it

Part IV: Below is the story you just heard.   Fill in the
blanks with the appropriate word.

Alice stood waiting near _____ cash register in

the _____ wear department.   After the _____ had

finished waiting on _____ customer, she turned to

_____.   Handing her a box, _____ explained that

she wanted _____ return a blouse that _____ been

given to her _____ a gift.   Although there _____

nothing wrong with the _____, Alice didn't want it

_____ it wasn't the right _____.   She

wanted a beige _____ but after checking the _____

the girl told her _____ it didn't come in _____.

Since Alice couldn't get _____ blouse in the color

_____ wanted, she decided to _____ a

refund.   Fortunately, the _____ recognized the tag

on _____ blouse so a receipt _____ necessary.

19

Alice Studies a Restaurant Menu

Part I: Look over the following sentences and make sure
            that you understand the words and the meaning of
            each sentence.

_____ A.   "We'll need a few more minutes, miss," continued
            Mark, turning to the waitress. "We haven't quite
            made up our minds."

_____ B.   "Oh, I don't really want a drink," Mark replied as
            he studied the menu. "I think I'm about ready to
            order."

_____ C.   "I'm afraid I'm not," Alice answered, turning to
            the others, "but you two go ahead and order while
            I try to decide."

_____ D.   "No, I don't think so," Mary replied. "A drink
            before dinner usually makes me sleepy."

_____ E.   "Oh, I don't think she was upset," Mark said. "And
            besides, if she's not pleasant we won't leave her
            a big tip."

_____ F.   "The beef stroganoff," Alice repeated. "I don't
            think I want that. What are you having, Mark?"

_____ G.   "There's no need to rush, Alice," Mark responded.
            "Just take your time."

_____ H.   "Would you like a drink before we order?" asked
            Mark as he opened his menu.

_____ I.   "The sirloin steak--you know me, I love steak,"
            Mark replied as he noticed the waitress coming
            toward them.

_____ J.   "I don't think I want one either," Alice added,
            looking up from her menu. "But you go ahead, Mark,
            and order one. Don't let us stop you."

_____ K.   "Are you ready to order?" the waitress asked,
            glancing around the table.

_____ L.   "Oh, gosh," Alice said as she watched the waitress
            walk away. "She seemed annoyed. I hope I haven't
            made her angry."

_____ M.   "Me too," Mary answered, closing the menu. "I think
            the beef stroganoff sounds good."

Check the appropriate answer to each question
after it is read to you.

1. ___ Yes, she did.   4. ___ Yes, he did.
   ___ No, Mary did.   ___ Yes, he was.
   ___ No, she didn't.   ___ No, he didn't.

2. ___ Yes, she did.   5. ___ Yes, he did.
   ___ Yes, she had.   ___ No, he didn't.
   ___ No, Mary did.   ___ Yes, he had.

3. ___ Yes, she did.
   ___ No, she hadn't.
   ___ No, she didn't.

Part III: Listen to the reading passage and then check the
            appropriate answer to each question.

1. ___ A. because Mark didn't
   ___ B. because it might make her sleepy
   ___ C. because she was ready to order

2. ___ A. the beef stroganoff
   ___ B. the sirloin steak
   ___ C. a drink before dinner

3. ___ A. Alice was but Mark wasn't
   ___ B. Mark was but Mary wasn't
   ___ C. both Mary and Mark were

4. ___ A. to go ahead and order
   ___ B. that the waitress was upset
   ___ C. to take her time

5. ___ A. because Mary wanted the beef stroganoff
   ___ B. because she told the others to go ahead and order
   ___ C. because she wasn't ready to order

Part IV: Below is the story you just heard. Fill in the blanks with the appropriate word.

Mark opened his menu _____ then asked Alice and

_____ if they would like _____ drink before

they ordered _____. Mary didn't want one _____

it would make her _____ and Alice didn't want

_____ either. However, she urged _____ to

order a drink _____ he wanted one. Mark _____

was about ready to _____ and he didn't really

_____ a drink. Mary decided _____ beef

stroganoff sounded good _____ Mark wanted a sirloin

_____. When the waitress came _____ take

their orders, Alice _____ still not sure what

_____ wanted. She told the _____ to go

ahead and _____ but Mark told her _____ take

her time and _____ the waitress for a _____

more minutes. Alice was _____ the waitress was

angry _____ of this but Mark _____ think she

was upset. _____, he told Alice, if _____

waitress wasn't pleasant they _____ leave her a

big tip.

Alice Complains About Her Car Insurance

Part I: Look over the following sentences and make sure
that you understand the words and the meaning of
each sentence.

_____ A. "Why sure," Mary answered. "If you have too many
claims they raise your rates and you end up paying
more."

_____ B. "No, I paid the premium," Alice replied. "It's
just that I didn't know that my policy was $100
deductible."

_____ C. "Come on in and sit down, Alice, you look upset,"
Mary said. "What's the matter?"

_____ D. "All three under $100," Mary repeated sympatheti-
cally. "Well, look on the bright side, Alice, at
least they won't raise your rates."

_____ E. "It sounded like a crash," Mary answered as she and
Alice ran to the window. "Oh no, Alice, somebody
just hit your car."

_____ F. "Oh, it's my darn car insurance," Alice answered.
"My agent just told me they won't pay for my dented
fender."

_____ G. "What do you mean, raise my rates?" Alice asked.
"They couldn't do that, could they?"

_____ H. "Paying more," Alice repeated thoughtfully. "That's
not fair--hey, what was that sound?"

_____ I. "Oh, I see," said Mary, "that little dent won't
cost more than $100 to fix so the insurance company
isn't going to pay."

_____ J. "They won't?" Mary responded. "Why not? You
didn't forget to pay the premium, did you?"

_____ K. "Oh my gosh," Alice laughed. "What luck! They hit
my dented fender."

_____ L. "That's right. Not a penny," Alice answered. "I
got three estimates and they were all just under
$100."

Part II: Check the appropriate answer to each question
after it is read to you.

1. ___ Yes, she was.   4. ___ Yes, they were.
   ___ Yes, she did.   ___ No, they weren't.
   ___ Yes, she had.   ___ Yes, they had.

2. ___ Yes, she did.   5. ___ Yes, it was.
   ___ No, she wasn't.   ___ No, it wasn't.
   ___ No, she didn't.   ___ Yes, it did.

3. ___ Yes, they were.
   ___ No, they weren't.
   ___ No, there weren't.

Part III: Listen to the reading passage and then check the
appropriate answer to each question.

1. ___ A. because they would raise her rates if she had too
              many claims
   ___ B. because somebody hit her dented fender
   ___ C. because her car insurance wouldn't pay for her
              dented fender

2. ___ A. if she had a dented fender
   ___ B. if she had too many claims
   ___ C. if she had $100 deductible

3. ___ A. because somebody hit her dented fender
   ___ B. because her policy was $100 deductible
   ___ C. because she had too many claims

4. ___ A. to see a crash
   ___ B. because they heard a crash
   ___ C. to see Alice's dented fender

5. ___ A. her dented fender had been hit
   ___ B. her car had been hit
   ___ C. they had heard a crash

80

Below is the story you just heard. Fill in the blanks with the appropriate word.

   Alice was upset when _____ came to Mary's

house _____ her insurance agent had _____ her

that her car _____ wouldn't pay for her _____

fender. Although Alice had _____ her premium, they

wouldn't _____ for her fender because _____

policy was $100 deductible. _____ had gotten three

estimates _____ they were all under _____

hundred dollars. Mary was _____ but said that at

_____ they wouldn't be raising _____ rates.

Alice didn't know _____ her insurance company could

_____ her rates if she _____ too many claims.

While _____ and Mary were talking, _____ heard

a sound like _____ crash. When they ran _____

the window, Mary saw _____ somebody had hit Alice's

_____. Alice had to laugh _____ she saw that

the _____ had hit her dented fender.

Alice Goes to a Garage Sale

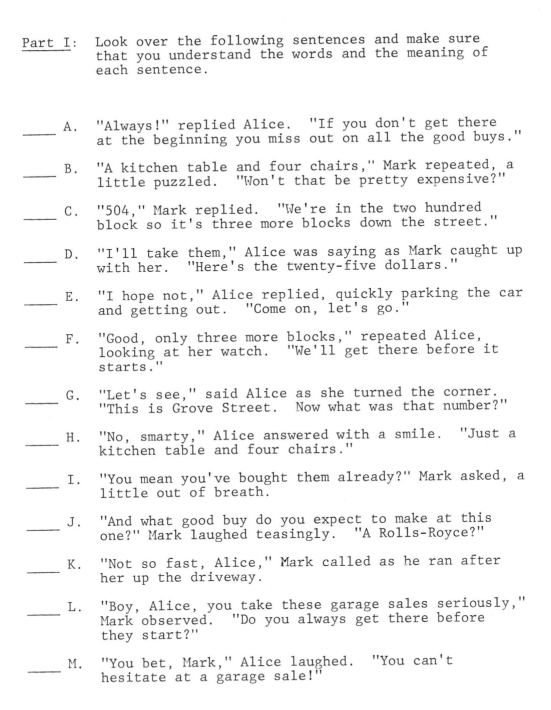

Part I: Look over the following sentences and make sure
that you understand the words and the meaning of
each sentence.

_____ A. "Always!" replied Alice. "If you don't get there
at the beginning you miss out on all the good buys."

_____ B. "A kitchen table and four chairs," Mark repeated, a
little puzzled. "Won't that be pretty expensive?"

_____ C. "504," Mark replied. "We're in the two hundred
block so it's three more blocks down the street."

_____ D. "I'll take them," Alice was saying as Mark caught up
with her. "Here's the twenty-five dollars."

_____ E. "I hope not," Alice replied, quickly parking the car
and getting out. "Come on, let's go."

_____ F. "Good, only three more blocks," repeated Alice,
looking at her watch. "We'll get there before it
starts."

_____ G. "Let's see," said Alice as she turned the corner.
"This is Grove Street. Now what was that number?"

_____ H. "No, smarty," Alice answered with a smile. "Just a
kitchen table and four chairs."

_____ I. "You mean you've bought them already?" Mark asked, a
little out of breath.

_____ J. "And what good buy do you expect to make at this
one?" Mark laughed teasingly. "A Rolls-Royce?"

_____ K. "Not so fast, Alice," Mark called as he ran after
her up the driveway.

_____ L. "Boy, Alice, you take these garage sales seriously,"
Mark observed. "Do you always get there before
they start?"

_____ M. "You bet, Mark," Alice laughed. "You can't
hesitate at a garage sale!"

Check the appropriate answer to each question
after it is read to you.

1. ___ No, Mark did.
   ___ No, she didn't.
   ___ Yes, she did.

4. ___ No, just twenty-five
       dollars.
   ___ Yes, she did.
   ___ No, Mark did.

2. ___ Yes, he did.
   ___ No, Alice did.
   ___ No, he didn't.

5. ___ Yes, he did.
   ___ Yes, he said that.
   ___ No, Alice said that.

3. ___ No, she didn't.
   ___ Yes, and four chairs.
   ___ No, Mark did.

Part III: Listen to the reading passage and then check the
appropriate answer to each question.

1. ___ A. three more blocks
   ___ B. on Grove Street
   ___ C. where they turned

2. ___ A. that they would get there before it started
   ___ B. that a garage sale was serious business
   ___ C. that they had three more blocks to go

3. ___ A. to see it start
   ___ B. to look at her watch
   ___ C. to get a good buy

4. ___ A. parked the car
   ___ B. bought the table and chairs
   ___ C. driven up the driveway

5. ___ A. because Mark caught up with her
   ___ B. because she wanted to surprise Mark
   ___ C. because you can't hesitate at a garage sale

84

Part IV: Below is the story you just heard. Fill in the
blanks with the appropriate word.

Alice and Mark were _____ to a garage sale.

_____ they turned onto Grove _____ Mark told

Alice that _____ had three more blocks _____ go

to reach 504. _____ looked at her watch _____

was pleased to see _____ they would get to _____

sale before it started. _____ Mark was surprised

how _____ Alice took garage sales, _____

explained that it was _____ to get there early

_____ get the good buys. _____ this

sale Alice hoped _____ buy a kitchen table

_____ four chairs. As soon _____ she had

parked the _____, Alice got out and _____

up the driveway. By _____ time Mark had caught

_____ with her, she had _____ bought the

table and _____ for twenty-five dollars. Mark was

_____ she had acted so _____ but Alice

explained that _____ never hesitated at a

_____ sale.

85

Alice Gets Her Car Started
with Jumper Cables

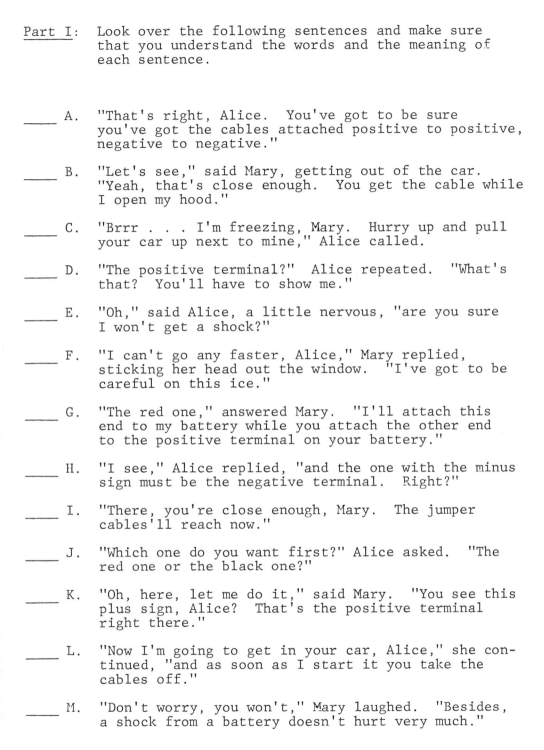

Part I: Look over the following sentences and make sure that you understand the words and the meaning of each sentence.

_____ A. "That's right, Alice. You've got to be sure you've got the cables attached positive to positive, negative to negative."

_____ B. "Let's see," said Mary, getting out of the car. "Yeah, that's close enough. You get the cable while I open my hood."

_____ C. "Brrr . . . I'm freezing, Mary. Hurry up and pull your car up next to mine," Alice called.

_____ D. "The positive terminal?" Alice repeated. "What's that? You'll have to show me."

_____ E. "Oh," said Alice, a little nervous, "are you sure I won't get a shock?"

_____ F. "I can't go any faster, Alice," Mary replied, sticking her head out the window. "I've got to be careful on this ice."

_____ G. "The red one," answered Mary. "I'll attach this end to my battery while you attach the other end to the positive terminal on your battery."

_____ H. "I see," Alice replied, "and the one with the minus sign must be the negative terminal. Right?"

_____ I. "There, you're close enough, Mary. The jumper cables'll reach now."

_____ J. "Which one do you want first?" Alice asked. "The red one or the black one?"

_____ K. "Oh, here, let me do it," said Mary. "You see this plus sign, Alice? That's the positive terminal right there."

_____ L. "Now I'm going to get in your car, Alice," she continued, "and as soon as I start it you take the cables off."

_____ M. "Don't worry, you won't," Mary laughed. "Besides, a shock from a battery doesn't hurt very much."

87

Part II: Check the appropriate answer to each question
after it is read to you.

1. ___ Yes, she did.   4. ___ Yes, it was.
   ___ No, she didn't.   ___ No, it wasn't.
   ___ Yes, she was.   ___ No, it shouldn't.

2. ___ Yes, she did.   5. ___ Yes, she was.
   ___ No, to the positive.   ___ Yes, she did.
   ___ No, she hadn't.   ___ No, Alice was.

3. ___ Yes, it was.
   ___ No, it wasn't.
   ___ Yes, the positive.

Part III: Listen to the reading passage and then check the
appropriate answer to each question.

1. ___ A. because Alice's car wouldn't start
   ___ B. because there was ice
   ___ C. because Alice was waiting in the cold

2. ___ A. she got the jumper cables
   ___ B. she attached the jumper cables
   ___ C. she started her car

3. ___ A. to the positive terminal of her battery
   ___ B. to the negative terminal of her battery
   ___ C. to the minus sign on her battery

4. ___ A. attach the jumper cables
   ___ B. find the negative terminal
   ___ C. take the jumper cables off

5. ___ A. she wouldn't know what the positive terminal was
   ___ B. she would get a shock
   ___ C. her car wouldn't start

Part IV: Below is the story you just heard. Fill in the
         blanks with the appropriate word.

Alice stood waiting in _____ cold for Mary to

_____ her car up next _____ hers. Mary

had to _____ carefully because there was _____

but she soon had _____ car close enough to _____

so they could connect _____ jumper cables. While

Alice _____ the cables, Mary opened _____

hood. First Mary attached _____ red cable to her

_____ and then she told _____ to attach the

other _____ of the cable to _____ positive

terminal of Alice's _____. Since Alice didn't know

_____ the positive terminal was, _____ had to

attach it. _____ showed Alice the plus _____ on

the battery next _____ the positive terminal. Alice

_____ guessed that the minus _____ was for

the negative _____. Mary said that Alice _____

to be sure she _____ the cables attached positive

_____ positive, negative to negative. _____

she told Alice to _____ the cables off as _____

as she started Alice's _____. Alice, however, was

afraid _____ might get a shock.

89

Alice Buys a Birthday Card

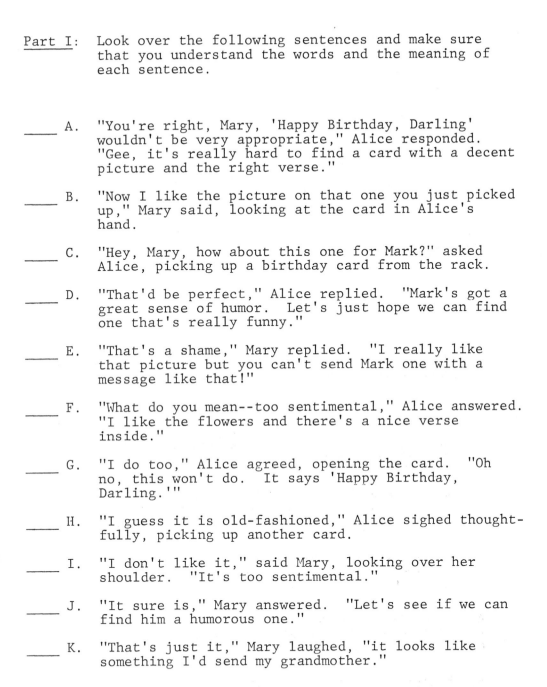

Part I: Look over the following sentences and make sure
          that you understand the words and the meaning of
          each sentence.

_____ A.   "You're right, Mary, 'Happy Birthday, Darling'
           wouldn't be very appropriate," Alice responded.
           "Gee, it's really hard to find a card with a decent
           picture and the right verse."

_____ B.   "Now I like the picture on that one you just picked
           up," Mary said, looking at the card in Alice's
           hand.

_____ C.   "Hey, Mary, how about this one for Mark?" asked
           Alice, picking up a birthday card from the rack.

_____ D.   "That'd be perfect," Alice replied. "Mark's got a
           great sense of humor. Let's just hope we can find
           one that's really funny."

_____ E.   "That's a shame," Mary replied. "I really like
           that picture but you can't send Mark one with a
           message like that!"

_____ F.   "What do you mean--too sentimental," Alice answered.
           "I like the flowers and there's a nice verse
           inside."

_____ G.   "I do too," Alice agreed, opening the card. "Oh
           no, this won't do. It says 'Happy Birthday,
           Darling.'"

_____ H.   "I guess it is old-fashioned," Alice sighed thought-
           fully, picking up another card.

_____ I.   "I don't like it," said Mary, looking over her
           shoulder. "It's too sentimental."

_____ J.   "It sure is," Mary answered. "Let's see if we can
           find him a humorous one."

_____ K.   "That's just it," Mary laughed, "it looks like
           something I'd send my grandmother."

91

Check the appropriate answer to each question
after it is read to you.

1. ___ Yes, she was.   4. ___ Yes, it was.
   ___ Yes, she did.   ___ No, it wasn't.
   ___ No, for Mark.   ___ No, it didn't.

2. ___ Yes, she did.   5. ___ Yes, he did.
   ___ No, she didn't.   ___ Yes, he was.
   ___ No, Mary did.   ___ Yes, he does.

3. ___ Yes, she did.
   ___ No, she didn't.
   ___ No, Alice did.

<u>Part III</u>: Listen to the reading passage and then check the
appropriate answer to each question.

1. ___ A. Alice thought it was old-fashioned
   ___ B. she thought it was too sentimental
   ___ C. the verse wasn't appropriate

2. ___ A. they liked the verse but not the picture
   ___ B. they liked the picture but not the message
   ___ C. they liked the flowers but not the picture

3. ___ A. it was too old-fashioned
   ___ B. it wasn't humorous
   ___ C. it used the word "darling"

4. ___ A. that they look for a humorous card
   ___ B. that Mark had a great sense of humor
   ___ C. that they find a card with a sentimental message

5. ___ A. because Mark wasn't sentimental
   ___ B. because Mark had a great sense of humor
   ___ C. because Mark was really funny

Below is the story you just heard. Fill in the
blanks with the appropriate word

    Alice and Mary stood _____ front of a rack

_____ birthday cards looking for _____ card for

Mark. Mary _____ like the first one _____

picked up because it _____ too sentimental. Although

Alice _____ the flowers and the _____ verse in

the card, _____ agreed with Mary that _____

card was old-fashioned. Another _____ Alice picked

up had _____ picture they both liked, _____

inside it said "Happy _____, Darling." Mary thought

it _____ a shame that the _____ wouldn't do

because the _____ was inappropriate. She suggested

_____ Alice that they look _____ a humorous

card. Alice _____ that a humorous one _____ be

perfect because Mark _____ a great sense of

_____. She only hoped they _____ find one

that was _____ funny.

93

CHAPTER

24

Alice Goes Shopping
in a Department Store

Look over the following sentences and make sure that you understand the words and the meaning of each sentence.

_____ A. "Dress shirts are sold according to neck size," the salesman answered politely. "Do you know the neck size you want?"

_____ B. "Oh, I see," replied the salesman sympathetically. "Well, you could guess at the size and if it doesn't fit you could bring it back."

_____ C. "Just take the escalator to the second floor and turn right," she answered. "There's a big sign that says 'Men's Wear'--you can't miss it."

_____ D. "A dress shirt or a sport shirt, ma'am?" the sales-man asked. "The dress shirts are right here and the sport shirts are behind you on that rack."

_____ E. "Well, ma'am, could you call and find out the neck size?" the salesman asked. "And you should get the sleeve length too."

_____ F. "Excuse me, miss, where's the Men's Wear depart-ment?" Alice asked the clerk at the jewelry counter.

_____ G. "Oh, I hate to give something that might not fit," Alice said thoughtfully. "Maybe I'd better take a look at the neckties."

_____ H. "The sleeve length too," Alice sighed unhappily. "This is getting more and more complicated. This shirt was going to be a birthday present."

_____ I. "I'd like to buy a shirt," Alice said as she walked up to the salesman behind the shirt counter.

_____ J. "I want a nice white dress shirt," Alice answered. "Something in a medium."

_____ K. "No, I don't," replied Alice. "I didn't realize I needed to know that."

Check the appropriate answer to each question
after it is read to you.

1. ___ Yes, she did.   4. ___ Yes, there were.
   ___ No, she didn't.   ___ Yes, they were.
   ___ Alice did.   ___ No, they weren't.
   ___ No, it was.

2. ___ Yes, it was.   5. ___ Yes, she did.
   ___ Yes, he was.   ___ No, the salesman did.
   ___ No, it wasn't.   ___ No, she didn't.

3. ___ Yes, she did.
   ___ No, she didn't.
   ___ No, not a white shirt.

Part III: Listen to the reading passage and then check the
            appropriate answer to each question.

1. ___ A. the jewelry counter was
   ___ B. the escalator was
   ___ C. the Men's Wear department was

2. ___ A. Alice took the escalator and turned right
   ___ B. Alice turned right and took the escalator
   ___ C. Alice followed the clerk in the jewelry
          department

3. ___ A. dress shirts were sold by neck size
   ___ B. she needed a medium in a dress shirt
   ___ C. the shirt was to be a birthday present

4. ___ A. exchange it for a medium
   ___ B. bring it back
   ___ C. buy a necktie

5. ___ A. she didn't want to give a white shirt as a present
   ___ B. she didn't find any medium dress shirts
   ___ C. she didn't like to give something that might
          not fit

Below is the story you just heard. Fill in the
blanks with the appropriate word.

Alice wanted to buy _____*a*_____ shirt for a birthday
___*present*___. She asked the clerk _____*at*_____ the jewelry
counter where ____*the*____ Men's Wear department was
___*located*___ then took the escalator _____*to*_____ the second
floor and ___*turned*___ right. She walked up ____*to*____ the
salesman behind the ___*shirt*___ counter and asked to
___*see*___ a white dress shirt ___*in*___ a medium. The
salesman ___*told*___ her however that dress ___*shirts*___
were sold according to ___*neck*___ size. Because Alice
didn't ___*know*___ the neck size she _____, he
suggested that she ___*try*___ and find out the ___*neck*___
size. At the same ___*time*___ she could find out ___*the*___
sleeve length too. However, ___*since*___ it was a birthday
___*present*___, Alice didn't want to ___*ask*___ the size.
The salesman ___*told*___ her she could guess ___*at*___ the
size and bring ___*back*___ shirt back if it ___*doesn't*___
fit. Alice decided to ___*look*___ at neckties instead
because ___*they*___ didn't like to give ___*something*___ that
might not fit.

Alice Eats Dinner with Her Friends

Part I: Look over the following sentences and make sure
         that you understand the words and the meaning of
         each sentence.

_____ A. "I wouldn't take that, Alice. You're a good cook,"
          Mary said, coming to Alice's defense.

_____ B. "Well Mark," Alice kidded, handing him the chicken,
          "you've had second helpings of everything. Are you
          going to have room for dessert?"

_3__ C.   "I'm glad you think so," Mary smiled. "I just hope
          everything tastes good."

_____ D. "I wish you could too," Mark teased, as he helped
          himself to some potatoes.

_1__ E.   "Gee, Mary, your table looks just beautiful,"
          Alice said as she sat down to eat.

_____ F. "Oh, I know I'm not a very good cook," Alice
          laughed as she passed Mark the corn.

_____ G. "I hope so," Mary observed. "We're having his
          favorite--banana cream pie."

_____ H. "It always does at your house," Alice responded.
          "Gosh, I wish I could cook like you, Mary."

_____ I. "Yes, thank you," answered Mark, "and I'll take
          just a little more of that fried chicken."

_____ J. "Oh, great!" Mark answered. "Does it have whipped
          cream on top?"

_2__ K.   "It sure does," Mark agreed, "and the food looks
          delicious."

_____ L. "Care for some more butter to put on that corn,
          Mark?" Mary asked.

Check the appropriate answer to each question
after it is read to you.

1. ___ Yes, he did.   4. ___ Yes, she did.
   ___ No, Mary did.   ___ Yes, but not corn.
   ___ No, Alice did.   ___ No, Mark did.

2. ___ Yes, he did.   5. ___ Yes, he was.
   ___ No, Mary did.   ___ No, Mary was.
   ___ No, they both did.   ___ Yes, he did.

3. ___ Yes, he did.
   ___ No, on his corn.
   ___ No, on his banana
       cream pie.

Part III: Listen to the reading passage and then check the
           appropriate answer to each question.

1. ___ A. that she could cook like Mary
   ___ B. that Mark would eat second helpings
   ___ C. that Mark would tease her

2. ___ A. because she could cook like Mary
   ___ B. because Alice agreed with Mark
   ___ C. because Mark teased Alice

3. ___ A. she knew she wasn't a good cook
   ___ B. she knew Mary was a good cook
   ___ C. she knew he wanted a second helping

4. ___ A. he knew Mary was a good cook
   ___ B. he wanted whipped cream on his pie
   ___ C. he had taken a second helping of everything

5. ___ A. because they were having his favorite dessert
   ___ B. because Alice kidded him
   ___ C. because she was a good cook

100

Part IV: Below is the story you just heard. Fill in the blanks with the appropriate word.

Alice and Mark had _____ invited to Mary's house _____ dinner. Mary hoped that _____ would taste good and _____ assured her that it _____ did at her house. _____, in fact, wished that _____ could cook like Mary. _____ teased Alice by saying _____ wished she could cook _____ Mary too. Mary came to the _____ of Alice's cooking but _____ laughingly agreed with Mark _____ she wasn't a very _____ cook. Since Mark wanted _____ second helping of everything, _____ kidded him that he _____ not have room for _____. Mary said she hoped _____ would because they were _____ Mark's favorite--banana cream _____. Mark was happy to _____ that and wanted to _____ if it would have _____ cream on top.

26

Alice Has a Complaint About Her Car

Part I: Look over the following sentences and make sure that you understand the words and the meaning of each sentence.

_____ A. "The carburetor? What's that got to do with it?" Alice asked.

_____ B. "Well, it's driving me crazy now," Alice sighed. "I've just got to get it fixed."

_____ C. "Oh, it's my car again," Alice complained. "It dies every time I pull up to a stop sign."

_____ D. "Well, a tune-up's not the answer to my problem. I had mine tuned up just last week."

_____ E. "Oh, you don't need to call a garage," Mary said. "Any good gas station attendant can adjust your carburetor."

_____ F. "Hi, Alice, why are you looking so glum?" Mary asked in a cheerful voice.

_____ G. "Mine was easy to fix," Mary continued. "I got a tune-up and after that it worked perfectly."

_____ H. "I'm not sure," Mary replied, "but I know if the carburetor's not adjusted correctly, a car will die when it's idling."

_____ I. "My car used to do that too," Mary answered sympathetically. "It drove me crazy."

_____ J. "I guess I'd better call the garage then and make an appointment to have it looked over," Alice sighed.

_____ K. "Maybe it's the carburetor then," Mary suggested.

103

Part II: Check the appropriate answer to each question
           after it is read to you.

1. ___ Yes, she did.   4. ___ Yes, it did.
   ___ Yes, she was.   ___ Yes, it was.
   ___ Yes, it did.   ___ Yes, she did.

2. ___ Yes, it did.   5. ___ Yes, she did.
   ___ No, it didn't.   ___ No, she didn't.
   ___ Yes, she did.   ___ No, she wasn't.

3. ___ Yes, it did.
   ___ Yes, it was.
   ___ No, it wasn't.

Part III: Listen to the reading passage and then check the
            appropriate answer to each question.

1. ___ A. it was dying every time she stopped
   ___ B. she needed a tune-up
   ___ C. she was going to call the garage

2. ___ A. because her car worked perfectly
   ___ B. because she had had the same trouble
   ___ C. because her carburetor needed adjusting

3. ___ A. it worked perfectly
   ___ B. she didn't have any more trouble
   ___ C. her car continued to die

4. ___ A. make an appointment at a garage
   ___ B. ask a service station attendant to fix it
   ___ C. get a tune-up

5. ___ A. because she needed a tune-up
   ___ B. because her carburetor didn't work
   ___ C. because any good gas station attendant could
           fix it

104

Part IV: Below is the story you just heard. Fill in the
blanks with the appropriate word.

Alice complained to her _____ Mary that she was

_____ trouble with her car-- _____ was dying

every time _____ stopped. Mary sympathized with

_____ because she had had _____ same trouble

with her _____. She said that Alice's _____

might be fixed by _____ tune-up. But Alice _____

a tune-up wasn't _____ answer because she had

_____ had her car tuned _____. When Mary

suggested that _____ might be the carburetor

_____ was causing the trouble, _____ thought

that maybe she _____ make an appointment at _____

garage to have her _____ looked over. Mary told

_____, however, that any good _____ station

attendant could adjust _____ carburetor so an

appointment _____ a garage wasn't necessary.

Alice Buys a Dress On Sale

Look over the following sentences and make sure that you understand the words and the meaning of each sentence.

_____ A. "Because it was still too expensive," Alice laughed. "But now they've got it marked down 50% and I can finally afford it."

_____ B. "I guess I might as well," Alice replied doubtfully, walking toward the fitting rooms.

_____ C. "I've been watching the price of that dress for over two months now," she added.

_____ D. Alice and Mary stopped to look in the window of their favorite dress shop.

_____ E. As they reached the rack with the sale dresses, Alice's face fell.

_____ F. In a minute she walked out beaming. "Look, Mary," she said. "It fits perfectly. I won't even have to take up the hem."

_____ G. "First they marked it down 10%, then 20%, and two weeks ago it was one-third off."

_____ H. "Why don't you try it on in a size larger, Alice?" Mary suggested. "You never know, it might fit."

_____ I. "Well, why didn't you buy it then when it was one-third off?" Mary asked.

_____ J. "Oh, that's great!" Alice said excitedly. "That's the dress I've been wanting and it's been reduced again."

_____ K. "Oh, no," she sighed, "they don't have it left in my size."

_____ L. "Well, if you're sure you can afford it, let's go in so you can try it on," Mary said.

Check the appropriate answer to each question
after it is read to you.

1. ___ Yes, it was.
   ___ Yes, she was.
   ___ No, she wasn't.

2. ___ Yes, it was.
   ___ No, 10%.
   ___ No, 50%.

3. ___ Yes, it could.
   ___ Yes, she could.
   ___ Yes, it was.

4. ___ Yes, she did.
   ___ No, in a size larger.
   ___ No, in her size.

5. ___ Yes, she would.
   ___ No, she wouldn't.
   ___ No, it would.

Part III: Listen to the reading passage and then check the
appropriate answer to each question.

1. ___ A. because the dress she wanted was in her size
   ___ B. because the dress she wanted was reduced again
   ___ C. because the dress she wanted was not on the rack

2. ___ A. because it was still too expensive
   ___ B. because it wasn't left in her size
   ___ C. because she had been watching it for two months

3. ___ A. when it was first marked down
   ___ B. when it was one-third off
   ___ C. when it was 50% off

4. ___ A. that the dress had been reduced again
   ___ B. that they didn't have the dress left in her size
   ___ C. that Mary had it in a smaller size

5. ___ A. because the dress fit perfectly
   ___ B. because they had it in a larger size
   ___ C. because she would have to take up the hem

108

Part IV: Below is the story you just heard.   Fill in the
           blanks with the appropriate word.

     When Alice and Mary _____ to look in the

_____ of their favorite dress _____, Alice was

excited to _____ that the dress she _____ been

wanting had been _____ again.   She told Mary

_____ she had been watching _____ price of the

dress _____ over two months.   Although _____

store had marked it _____ first 10%, then 20%

_____ finally one-third, it _____ still been

too expensive _____ her.   But when Alice _____

that it had been _____ 50%, she knew she _____

finally afford it.   Mary _____ that they go inside

_____ Alice could try it _____.   However,

when they reached _____ rack of sale dresses,

_____ saw that they didn't _____ it left in

her _____.   Mary suggested that she _____ it

on in a _____ larger and although Alice _____

that it would fit, _____ guessed she'd try it

_____.   To her surprise it _____ perfectly

and she wouldn't _____ have to take up _____

hem.

28

Alice Is Involved in a Collision

Part I: Look over the following sentences and make sure that you understand the words and the meaning of each sentence.

_____ A. "Yes, he did. He said I'd started to turn and I hit him," Alice exclaimed.

_____ B. "The policeman gave me the ticket," Alice cried angrily, "but I'm not going to pay it. I'm going to court."

_____ C. "What happened? Did somebody hit you?" Mary asked Alice, looking at her dented fender.

_____ D. "Well, what's his story? Did he try to say it was your fault?"

_____ E. "Yes," Alice replied. "I was in an intersection waiting to make a left turn when a car coming from the opposite direction turned in front of me and hit my fender."

_____ F. "You see," she added, "I found a witness who saw the whole thing and he'll swear I'm right."

_____ G. "That's exactly what he said," Alice replied. "He's trying to put the blame on me."

_____ H. "Now let me get this all straight," Mary said. "You were stopped and he was coming toward you when he turned left and hit the front of your car."

_____ I. "Oh, he said you were moving and that makes it look like you hit him," Mary responded.

_____ J. "That's right," said Alice, "that's the way it happened, but the man has a different story."

_____ K. "Well, if he blamed you and you blamed him, who got the ticket?" Mary asked.

Check the appropriate answer to each question after it is read to you.

1. ___ Yes, it was.
   ___ No, it wasn't.
   ___ Yes, it did.

2. ___ Yes, it was.
   ___ No, it wasn't.
   ___ Yes, she was.

3. ___ Yes, she did.
   ___ No, she didn't.
   ___ Yes, he did.

4. ___ Yes, he did.
   ___ Yes, he was.
   ___ No, Alice did.

5. ___ Yes, he will.
   ___ No, he won't.
   ___ No, the policeman will.

Part III: Listen to the reading passage and then check the appropriate answer to each question.

1. ___ A. to make a left turn
   ___ B. to hit the car coming from the opposite direction
   ___ C. to see her dented front fender

2. ___ A. that he had turned in front of Alice
   ___ B. that Alice had started to turn and hit him
   ___ C. that a witness had seen everything

3. ___ A. she was going to pay it
   ___ B. she wasn't going to pay it
   ___ C. she was going to give it to the witness

4. ___ A. because she had hit the man
   ___ B. because she had started to turn left
   ___ C. because she had found a witness

5. ___ A. that the policeman was right
   ___ B. that the man was right
   ___ C. that Alice was right

Part IV: Below is the story you just heard. Fill in the blanks with the appropriate word.

When Mary saw Alice's _____ fender she wanted

to _____ what had happened. According _____

Alice she had been _____ an intersection waiting to

_____ a left turn when _____ car coming from the

_____ direction turned in front _____ her.

When he turned _____ hit her front fender. _____

was sure this was _____ way it had happened, _____

the man had a _____ story. He said that _____

had started to turn _____ that she had hit _____.

He had blamed Alice _____ the policeman had given

_____ a ticket. Alice, however, _____ not

going to pay _____ ticket. She was going _____

court because she had _____ a witness who had

_____ everything and was going _____ swear

she was right.

Alice Helps Mark Rent an Apartment

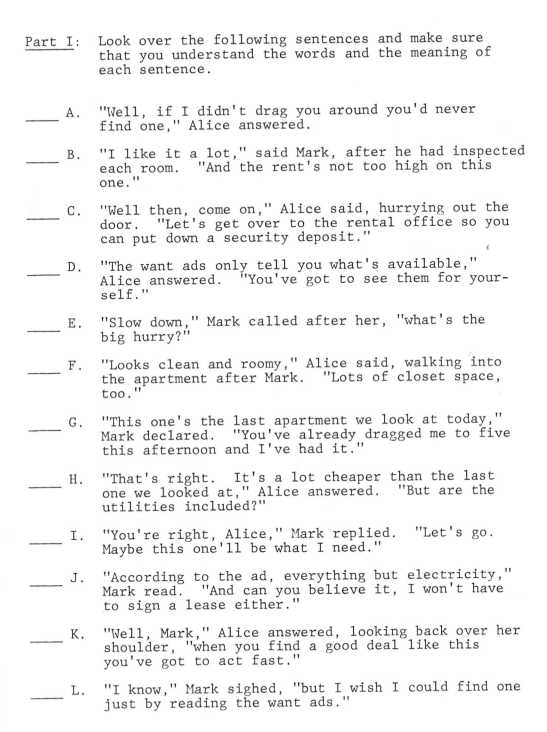

Part I: Look over the following sentences and make sure that you understand the words and the meaning of each sentence.

___ A. "Well, if I didn't drag you around you'd never find one," Alice answered.

___ B. "I like it a lot," said Mark, after he had inspected each room. "And the rent's not too high on this one."

___ C. "Well then, come on," Alice said, hurrying out the door. "Let's get over to the rental office so you can put down a security deposit."

___ D. "The want ads only tell you what's available," Alice answered. "You've got to see them for yourself."

___ E. "Slow down," Mark called after her, "what's the big hurry?"

___ F. "Looks clean and roomy," Alice said, walking into the apartment after Mark. "Lots of closet space, too."

___ G. "This one's the last apartment we look at today," Mark declared. "You've already dragged me to five this afternoon and I've had it."

___ H. "That's right. It's a lot cheaper than the last one we looked at," Alice answered. "But are the utilities included?"

___ I. "You're right, Alice," Mark replied. "Let's go. Maybe this one'll be what I need."

___ J. "According to the ad, everything but electricity," Mark read. "And can you believe it, I won't have to sign a lease either."

___ K. "Well, Mark," Alice answered, looking back over her shoulder, "when you find a good deal like this you've got to act fast."

___ L. "I know," Mark sighed, "but I wish I could find one just by reading the want ads."

115

Check the appropriate answer to each question
after it is read to you.

1. ___ Yes, she did.
   ___ No, he dragged her.
   ___ No, she didn't.

2. ___ Yes, she did.
   ___ No, she didn't.
   ___ Yes, there was.

3. ___ Yes, it was.
   ___ No, it wasn't.
   ___ No, he wasn't.

4. ___ Yes, that's right.
   ___ No, only electricity.
   ___ No, they weren't.

5. ___ Yes, he did.
   ___ No, he didn't.
   ___ Yes, she did.

Part III: Listen to the reading passage and then check the
appropriate answer to each question.

1. ___ A. five
   ___ B. only one more
   ___ C. the ones he wanted

2. ___ A. that it wasn't cheaper
   ___ B. that the utilities were included
   ___ C. that it looked clean and roomy

3. ___ A. because he wouldn't have to sign a lease
   ___ B. because it was cheaper
   ___ C. because the electricity wasn't included

4. ___ A. look at the apartment
   ___ B. sign a lease
   ___ C. put down a security deposit

5. ___ A. because it was a good deal
   ___ B. because the electricity wasn't included
   ___ C. because the apartment was clean and roomy

Below is the story you just heard. Fill in the
blanks with the appropriate word.

Alice had dragged Mark _____ look at five apart-

ments _____ he declared that he'd _____ it and

would only _____ at one more. He _____ that

this last apartment _____ were going to look _____

would be what he _____. Alice said it looked

_____ and roomy and it _____ lots of closet

space, _____. After he had inspected _____

the rooms, Mark said _____ liked it a lot _____

was pleased that the _____ wasn't too high. Alice

_____ that the apartment was _____ lot

cheaper than the _____ one they had looked _____

but she wanted to _____ if the utilities were

_____. According to the ad _____ all were

except electricity _____ Mark was surprised that

_____ wouldn't even have to _____ a lease.

Alice tried _____ hurry him over to _____

rental office so he _____ put down a security

_____. Mark thought she should _____ down,

but Alice knew _____ after finding such a _____

deal they had to _____ fast.

30

Alice Experiences a Power Outage

Part I: Look over the following sentences and make sure that you understand the words and the meaning of each sentence.

_____ A. "Just stay calm," Mary replied. "They'll probably come back on in a second."

_____ B. "Oh, just in time," Alice sighed, lighting the first candle. "There they go again."

_____ C. "Not this time," Mary answered. "I just saw a tree branch fall on the power line."

_____ D. "Oh, no, there go the lights!" Alice cried. "It's pitch dark in here."

_____ E. "I'll go with you," Alice cried. "I don't want to be alone if they go off again."

_____ F. "Well, go ahead and light the rest of the candles," Mary suggested. "I'm going to call the power company."

_____ G. "Just wait a second," Mary replied. "The next time there's a flash of lightning you'll see it too."

_____ H. "See, what did I tell you," Mary laughed. "Now just relax. I'm going to find some candles."

_____ I. "Come on then," Mary answered, hurrying to the kitchen. "You find some matches. I'll get the candles."

_____ J. "How could you see that?" Alice asked, staring out the kitchen window. "It's so dark out there."

_____ K. "Stay calm!" Alice exclaimed. "With this thunder and lightning! I can't stay . . . oh, there they are."

_____ L. "The power company?" Alice repeated, a little surprised. "Why not just wait and see if they come back on?"

Check the appropriate answer to each question after it is read to you.

1. ___ No, they didn't.
   ___ Yes, it did.
   ___ Yes, they did.

4. ___ Yes, she did.
   ___ No, she hadn't.
   ___ Yes, she had.

2. ___ Yes, she did.
   ___ No, he didn't.
   ___ No, she didn't.

5. ___ Yes, she did.
   ___ No, Mary did.
   ___ Yes, she had.

3. ___ Yes, she did.
   ___ No, Alice did.
   ___ Yes, they did.

Part III: Listen to the reading passage and then check the appropriate answer to each question.

1. ___ A. the tree branch
   ___ B. the lightning and thunder
   ___ C. the dark

2. ___ A. because she didn't want to be alone in the dark
   ___ B. in case the lights went out again
   ___ C. to see the tree branch that had fallen across the power line

3. ___ A. there was lightning and thunder
   ___ B. the lights had gone out
   ___ C. they found the matches

4. ___ A. got the matches
   ___ B. called the power company
   ___ C. waited in the kitchen

5. ___ A. there was lightning and thunder
   ___ B. Mary and Alice needed candles
   ___ C. a tree branch had fallen on the power line

120

Part IV: Below is the story you just heard.   Fill in the
         blanks with the appropriate word.

Alice was frightened by _____ lightning and

thunder and _____ couldn't stay calm when _____

lights went out. Although _____ came back on in

_____ minute, Mary suggested that _____ find

some candles in _____ the lights went out _____.

Not wanting to be _____ in the dark, Alice

_____ with Mary to the _____ and got some

matches. _____ that moment the lights _____

out again and Alice _____ some candles. Mary

reached _____ the phone to call _____ power

company. She knew _____ the lights would stay

_____ for a long time _____ a tree branch

had _____ across her power line. _____

reported the power outage _____ Alice stared out the

_____ waiting for the next _____ of lightning

so she _____ see the tree branch.

121

Alice Inquires About a Stove
Advertised in the Paper

Part I: Look over the following sentences and make sure that you understand the words and the meaning of each sentence.

_____ A. "That sounds like what I've been looking for," said Alice. "May I ask how much you want for it?"

_____ B. Hurrying to the door, Alice stopped suddenly. "Oh no," she sighed to herself. "I forgot to get her address."

_____ C. "Oh good," replied Alice. "It says in your ad that it's electric--is it in working order?"

_____ D. "Would it be okay if I came over right away?" Alice asked.

_____ E. "Oh my yes," answered Mrs. Wright. "It works just fine. It's fairly new and it's got a big self-cleaning oven."

_____ F. "Hello," said Alice, "I'm calling about the stove you've got advertised in the paper. Has it been sold yet?"

_____ G. "Sure," replied the woman, "if you can get here before five. I'll be out after that."

_____ H. "Hello, Mrs. Wright speaking," said the voice on the telephone.

_____ I. "Well, we're only asking $125 so if you're interested in it you'd better come over soon. I think it'll go fast."

_____ J. "No, ma'am," Mrs. Wright answered. "A couple of people are planning to come look at it later, but no one's bought it yet."

_____ K. "Oh, I can be there in ten minutes," Alice answered excitedly and hung up the phone.

123

Check the appropriate answer to each question
after it is read to you.

1. ___ Yes, it was.
   ___ No, it was fairly new.
   ___ No, it was very old.

2. ___ Yes, she was.
   ___ Yes, it was.
   ___ No, only $125

3. ___ Yes, she was.
   ___ No, after five.
   ___ No, in ten minutes.

4. ___ Yes, she did.
   ___ No, she didn't.
   ___ No, after five.

5. ___ Yes, she did.
   ___ No, she got it.
   ___ Yes, she had.

Part III: Listen to the reading passage and then check the
appropriate answer to each question.

1. ___ A. there was a stove advertised in the paper
   ___ B. the stove had not yet been sold
   ___ C. some people were planning to look at the stove

2. ___ A. what she had been looking for
   ___ B. not in working condition
   ___ C. big and self-cleaning

3. ___ A. it was advertised in the paper
   ___ B. it was fairly new
   ___ C. she was only asking $125 for it

4. ___ A. some people were planning to look at the stove
   ___ B. the woman would be out after 5:00
   ___ C. she thought the stove would sell fast

5. ___ A. the woman's address
   ___ B. the price of the stove
   ___ C. when the woman was going out

Below is the story you just heard. Fill in the
blanks with the appropriate word.

Alice called to ask _____ a stove advertised in

_____ paper. She was happy _____ hear that

although some _____ were planning to look _____

it, no one had _____ it yet. Alice wanted _____

know if it was _____ working condition. The woman

_____ her it worked fine _____ was fairly new

with _____ big self-cleaning oven. _____

thought that it sounded _____ what she had been

_____ for. Since the woman _____ only asking

$125 for _____ stove, she thought it _____

sell fast. Alice decided _____ go look at it

_____ the woman told her _____ get there

before five _____. It wasn't until after _____

had said she'd be _____ in ten minutes and

_____ hung up the phone _____ she realized

she didn't _____ the woman's address.

Alice Checks Out at the Grocery Store

Look over the following sentences and make sure that you understand the words and the meaning of each sentence.

_____ A. "I'm sorry to stop you again," Alice said politely, "but didn't you charge me 69¢ for the apples?"

_____ B. As her milk was being rung up, Alice noticed that the girl had charged her the regular price.

_____ C. Quickly ringing up the remaining items, she added the sales tax and said, "That'll be $26.42, ma'am."

_____ D. "I'll take the 24¢ off the cereal," she added, as she continued to ring up the groceries.

_____ E. When it was Alice's turn at the checkout counter, she handed the checkout girl three coupons.

_____ F. "Yes," said Alice, "I believe the milk's been reduced from $1.69 to $1.45."

_____ G. "Oh," said Alice, "I hate to mention it, but I'm afraid you forgot to take off for my coupons."

_____ H. "Pardon me," Alice said, "but isn't milk on special this week?"

_____ I. "You're right again, ma'am," the girl sighed as she checked the tape. "The apples are supposed to be 59¢ so I'll take ten cents off the cheese."

_____ J. Then she watched as the girl rang up her groceries.

_____ K. "Well, let's see," the girl said, "then that's 24¢ I overcharged you."

_____ L. "You're right, it is," the girl responded, "and I charged you the regular price, didn't I?"

Check the appropriate answer to each question
after it is read to you.

1. ___ Yes, it was.
   ___ No, the regular price.
   ___ No, it wasn't.

2. ___ No, for the cereal.
   ___ No, she didn't.
   ___ Yes, ten cents.

3. ___ Yes, she did.
   ___ No, off the milk.
   ___ Yes, she was.

4. ___ Yes, she did.
   ___ No, the girl did.
   ___ No, she hadn't.

5. ___ Yes, she did.
   ___ No, she wasn't.
   ___ No, the girl did.

Part III: Listen to the reading passage and then check the
appropriate answer to each question.

1. ___ A. the tape
   ___ B. the twenty-four cents she was overcharged
   ___ C. three coupons

2. ___ A. because she had overcharged her
   ___ B. because she had forgotten the coupons
   ___ C. because the cheese was on special

3. ___ A. because it was on special
   ___ B. because Alice had a coupon for it
   ___ C. because she had overcharged Alice for the milk

4. ___ A. she took off for the coupons
   ___ B. she added the sales tax
   ___ C. she overcharged for the apples

5. ___ A. that the total was $26.42
   ___ B. that the apples were on special
   ___ C. that she had forgotten to take off for the
          coupons

Part IV: Below is the story you just heard. Fill in the
blanks with the appropriate word.

Alice handed the girl _____ the checkout counter

three _____ and watched as the _____ rang up her

groceries. _____ her milk was being _____ up,

Alice noticed that _____ girl had charged the

_____ price. She stopped the _____ and

reminded her that _____ milk was on special _____

$1.45 and the girl _____ charged $1.69 instead.

The _____ took the twenty-four cents she _____

overcharged Alice off the _____. Alice had to stop

_____ again when she charged _____ for the

apples which _____ supposed to be 59¢. _____

she had finished ringing _____ all of Alice's

items _____ had added the sales _____, she

told Alice the _____ was $26.42. Alice, however,

_____ to mention to the _____ that she had

forgotten _____ take off for the _____.

Alice Finds an Error in Her Checkbook

Part I: Look over the following sentences and make sure that you understand the words and the meaning of each sentence.

_____ A. After a few minutes of checking the stubs, Mary cried, "I've got it. Here's your error."

_____ B. "Oh no, not $48," Alice sighed. "If that's the case, I'm sure I'm overdrawn."

_____ C. "Sure," Mary said, picking up the cancelled checks and looking through them. "Are all of these recorded?"

_____ D. "Oh, I see," said Alice, looking at the stub. "That was dumb of me. Now I've got $24 less than I thought I had."

_____ E. "What's wrong, Alice? You look worried," Mary asked sympathetically.

_____ F. "You're right, Alice, according to my figures you're overdrawn $7.45," Mary answered, putting down the check stubs.

_____ G. "Well then, maybe there's a mistake in your figuring," said Mary, reaching for the check stubs.

_____ H. "I'm having a hard time balancing my checkbook," Alice sighed. "Could you help me?"

_____ I. "Not $24 less," Mary answered. "You've got $48 less than you thought you had."

_____ J. "Come on then, Mary," Alice cried, picking up her purse. "I want to get to the bank and make a deposit before any of my checks bounce!"

_____ K. "Yes," answered Alice. "I'm very good about re-cording every check I write."

_____ L. "See, you added this check for $24 when you should've subtracted it."

Check the appropriate answer to each question after it is read to you.

1. ___ Yes, she was.
   ___ No, she wasn't.
   ___ Yes, she did.

2. ___ Yes, she was.
   ___ No, she wasn't.
   ___ Yes, they were.

3. ___ Yes, she was.
   ___ No, she wasn't.
   ___ Yes, she did.

4. ___ Yes, she did.
   ___ No, $48 less.
   ___ No, she didn't.

5. ___ Yes, she was.
   ___ Yes, she did.
   ___ No, Alice was.

Part III: Listen to the reading passage and then check the appropriate answer to each question.

1. ___ A. because she was going to the bank
   ___ B. because she had recorded all her checks
   ___ C. because she was having a hard time balancing her checkbook

2. ___ A. she had added when she should have subtracted
   ___ B. she had subtracted when she should have added
   ___ C. she had added $7.45

3. ___ A. $7.45
   ___ B. $48
   ___ C. $24

4. ___ A. because she had $48 less than she thought she had
   ___ B. because she didn't want her checks to bounce
   ___ C. because she had $24 less than she thought she had

5. ___ A. because she recorded every check she wrote
   ___ B. because she subtracted a check for $48
   ___ C. because she didn't want any of her checks to bounce

132

Part IV: Below is the story you just heard. Fill in the
blanks with the appropriate word.

    Alice was having a _____ time balancing her

checkbook _____ she asked Mary to _____ her.

Mary wanted to _____ if all of her _____ checks

had been recorded. _____ answered that she was

_____ good about recording every _____ she

wrote. When Mary _____ this, she thought that

_____ there was a mistake _____ Alice's

figuring. After looking _____ the check stubs, Mary

_____ the error. Alice had _____ a check

for $24 _____ she should have subtracted _____ .

This meant that Alice _____ $48 less than she

_____ she had. When Alice _____ this, she was

sure _____ was overdrawn. And according _____

Mary's figures Alice was _____ $7.45. Not wanting

any _____ her checks to bounce, _____ asked

Mary to come _____ her to the bank _____ she

could make a _____ .

Alice Looks for a Cold Remedy in the Drugstore

Part I: Look over the following sentences and make sure that you understand the words and the meaning of each sentence.

_____ A. "There are several kinds of decongestants to choose from," he added. "Each one works a little differently."

_____ B. "You can find the decongestants in Aisle B next to the cough remedies," he added as Alice turned away.

_____ C. Alice had been looking for some cold medicine in the drugstore but she couldn't find what she wanted.

_____ D. "Can you recommend some kind of non-prescription drug?" she added.

_____ E. "If you're stopped up then you need a decongestant," replied the pharmacist.

_____ F. "Some do," replied the pharmacist, "but many people find the twelve-hour kinds make their sinuses too dry."

_____ G. In the back of the store was a large sign that said "Pharmacy" so she decided to ask the pharmacist for help.

_____ H. "What are your symptoms, ma'am?" asked the pharmacist. "Do you need something for a cough?"

_____ I. "I need something for my cold," she said as she walked up to the counter.

_____ J. "No," said Alice. "I don't have much of a cough, but my nose is so stopped up that I can't breathe at night."

_____ K. "Do they all last for twelve hours?" asked Alice.

135

Check the appropriate answer to each question
after it is read to you.

1. ___ No, she couldn't.   4. ___ Yes, they do.
   ___ Yes, she could.   ___ No, only some do.
   ___ Yes, she can.   ___ Yes, they all do.

2. ___ Yes, there was.   5. ___ Yes, they were.
   ___ No, it said "Pharmacy."   ___ No, there were.
   ___ No, she wasn't.   ___ No, they weren't.

3. ___ Yes, she did.
   ___ No, she didn't.
   ___ No, the pharmacist did.

Part III: Listen to the reading passage and then check the
appropriate answer to each question.

1. ___ A. he was in the back of the store
   ___ B. he knew what her symptoms were
   ___ C. she wasn't sure what she wanted

2. ___ A. a non-prescription drug
   ___ B. a prescription drug
   ___ C. a cough remedy

3. ___ A. dry sinuses
   ___ B. a cough
   ___ C. a stopped-up nose

4. ___ A. it would make her sinuses too dry
   ___ B. her nose was stopped up
   ___ C. she didn't know what her symptoms were

5. ___ A. where the decongestants were
   ___ B. what her symptoms were
   ___ C. what kind of drug she wanted

Below is the story you just heard. Fill in the
blanks with the appropriate word.

    Alice went to the _____ to buy some medicine

_____ her cold. She wasn't _____ what she wanted

so _____ decided to ask the _____ in the back of

_____ store for help. When _____ told him she

wanted _____ non-prescription drug for _____

cold, he wanted to _____ what her symptoms were.

_____ first thought she needed _____ for a

cough but _____ problem was a stopped _____ nose

that made it _____ to breathe at night. _____

pharmacist suggested a decongestant _____ told Alice

there were _____ kinds to choose from. _____ ,

he added, could last for _____ hours but might dry

_____ the sinuses as well. _____ pharmacist

then told her _____ to find the decongestants,

_____ Alice would have to _____ for herself

which kind _____ wanted.

35

Alice Asks for Directions at a Gas Station

Part I: Look over the following sentences and make sure that you understand the words and the meaning of each sentence.

_____ A. "825 Jefferson," Alice said with a sigh. "I've been trying to find it for over half an hour."

_____ B. "Would you mind repeating it while I write it down?" she added, taking a pencil and pad out of her purse.

_____ C. Seeing an attendant standing next to the cash register, she walked inside.

_____ D. "At the stop you'll take a right onto Oak and go two blocks west until you come to Jefferson, which is one-way going north."

_____ E. "Oh," said Alice, "I'm afraid I can't remember all of that."

_____ F. "You wouldn't have a map of the city, by any chance, would you?" she asked.

_____ G. "You go left on Monroe for about ten blocks until you come to a four-way stop."

_____ H. Alice pulled into a gas station and got out of her car.

_____ I. "At Jefferson take another right and head north.

_____ J. "No, ma'am," he replied, "but I know just about every street in town. Where do you want to go?"

_____ K. "You'll cross Walnut, which is one-way going east, and the next block is the eight hundred block of Jefferson."

_____ L. "Well," the young man said, "this street in front of the station is Monroe."

139

Part II: Check the appropriate answer to each question
           after it is read to you.

1. ___ Yes, he did.   4. ___ Yes, she would.
   ___ Yes, he was.   ___ No, right.
   ___ No, he didn't.   ___ No, she did.

2. ___ Yes, he did.   5. ___ Yes, she would.
   ___ No, he didn't.   ___ No, east.
   ___ No, she asked him.   ___ Yes, she did.

3. ___ Yes, he did.
   ___ No, he didn't.
   ___ Yes, he was.

Part III: Listen to the reading passage and then check the
            appropriate answer to each question.

1. ___ A. to look for an attendant
   ___ B. to ask for a city map
   ___ C. to find Monroe Street

2. ___ A. north of Jefferson
   ___ B. north of Walnut
   ___ C. in front of the station

3. ___ A. go north
   ___ B. cross Walnut
   ___ C. turn right

4. ___ A. Walnut
   ___ B. Jefferson again
   ___ C. Monroe

5. ___ A. so she could write it down
   ___ B. because he didn't have a map
   ___ C. because he wouldn't mind

140

Part IV: Below is the story you just heard. Fill in the
blanks with the appropriate word.

    Alice pulled into a _____ station to ask for

_____ city map. The attendant _____ have a map

but _____ knew just about every _____ in town and

asked _____ she wanted to go. _____ told him

she had _____ trying to find 825 _____ . To

reach Jefferson the _____ told her to go _____

on Monroe, which was _____ street in front of

_____ station. After about ten _____ she

would come to _____ four-way stop. At _____

stop she was to _____ a right onto Oak _____

go two blocks west _____ Jefferson. At Jefferson

Alice _____ told to take a _____ and head

north. First _____ would cross Walnut and _____

next block would be _____ 800 block of Jefferson.

_____ Alice couldn't remember all _____ he had

said, she _____ him if he'd mind _____ it

while she wrote _____ down.

Alice Sees Her Car Hit

Part I: Look over the following sentences and make sure
          that you understand the words and the meaning of
          each sentence.

_2_ A.   "What's wrong, Alice?" Mary asked.

_6_ B.   "Couldn't I just give you my name and my insurance
          company and we'll settle this later?" the driver
          asked.

_4_ C.   As the women watched, the driver got out of his car
          and looked at the damage.

____ D.   Without waiting for his answer she added, "I think
          we'd better call the police."

____ E.   "Well, all right," the driver conceded, "but I'm
          sure my insurance company'll handle this without
          any problem."

____ F.   "Looks like you really dented in my front fender,"
          she said.

_1_ G.   "Oh, no!" Alice cried as she and her friend Mary
          walked into the parking lot.

____ H.   "I don't think it would be right to leave without
          calling the police, Alice," Mary said.

_5_ I.   Hurrying over to the accident scene, Alice spoke
          to the driver of the station wagon.

_3_ J.   "That red station wagon just backed into my car!"
          Alice exclaimed.

____ K.   "I agree, Mary, there's more than a hundred
          dollars' damage to my car and I'm sure the police
          are supposed to be notified."

143

Part II: Check the appropriate answer to each question
           after it is read to you.

1. ___ Yes it did.   4. ___ Yes, he did.
   ___ No, into Mary's car.   ___ No, Alice did.
   ___ No, it didn't.   ___ Yes, he had.

2. ___ Yes, he did.   5. ___ Yes, there was.
   ___ No, he got out.   ___ No, there was more.
   ___ No, he wasn't.   ___ Yes, it was.

3. ___ Yes, he was.
   ___ No, he wasn't.
   ___ Yes, it was.

Part III: Listen to the reading passage and then check the
            appropriate answer to each question.

1. ___ A. while she was driving into the parking lot
   ___ B. while it was parked in the parking lot
   ___ C. while the station wagon was parked in the
           parking lot

2. ___ A. left his name and insurance company
   ___ B. called the police
   ___ C. got out of his car and looked at the damage

3. ___ A. give Alice his name and insurance company
   ___ B. back into her front fender
   ___ C. call the police

4. ___ A. the driver had backed into her car in the parking
           lot
   ___ B. there was more than one hundred dollars' damage
   ___ C. the driver didn't know his insurance company

5. ___ A. look at the damage
   ___ B. handle it without any problem
   ___ C. make sure the police were called

144

Part IV: Below is the story you just heard.   Fill in the
blanks with the appropriate word.

As Alice was walking _____ her friend Mary into

_____ parking lot, she saw _____ red station

wagon back _____ her parked car.   The _____ of

the station wagon _____ out of his car _____

looked at the damage.   _____ hurried up to him

_____ said that they had _____ call the

police because _____ had really dented in _____

front fender.   The driver _____ to give Alice his

_____ and his insurance company _____

settle it later but _____ thought the police should

_____ called.   Alice agreed with _____

because there was more _____ one hundred dollars'

damage _____ her car.   The driver _____

reluctantly but assured them _____ his insurance

company would _____ it without any problem.

Alice Asks for Some Advice About Her Income Tax

Look over the following sentences and make sure that you understand the words and the meaning of each sentence.

____ A. "I don't need an expert," Alice responded. "I'm just using the short form."

____ B. "If I did get it," Alice sighed, "I don't know what I did with it."

____ C. "My W-2 form? Oh, you mean the form I got from work?"

____ D. "Here it is," Alice said, taking a form out of an envelope. "I've got three copies of it."

____ E. "Could you help me with my income tax return?" Alice asked Mary. "I've got to mail it in by the 15th."

____ F. "That's right, Alice, the one that tells how much you made and how much was withheld."

____ G. "Oh, don't worry," Mary reassured her. "We can get another one at the bank."

____ H. "Well, of course you've got to have the 1040 form. Didn't you get it in the mail?"

____ I. "Oh, the short form's a snap," Mary replied. "Now let's see, have you got your W-2 form?"

____ J. "You're supposed to," Mary agreed. "You send one copy in to the IRS, one to the state, and you keep the third."

____ K. "Sure, I can help you," Mary answered, "but I'm no expert."

____ L. "Don't I need something else besides my W-2's?" asked Alice.

Check the appropriate answer to each question after it is read to you.

1. ___ Yes, she was.
   ___ No, she wasn't.
   ___ Yes, they were.

2. ___ No, she didn't.
       Mary did.
   ___ Yes, she did.
   ___ Yes, Mary did.

3. ___ Yes, she did.
   ___ No, she didn't.
       Mary did.
   ___ No, they didn't.

4. ___ Yes, she did.
   ___ No, she didn't. Mary
       did.
   ___ No, she didn't.

5. ___ Yes, she did.
   ___ No, she didn't. Mary
       did.
   ___ No, they didn't.

Part III: Listen to the reading passage and then check the appropriate answer to each question.

1. ___ A. the short form was a snap
   ___ B. she couldn't find the 1040 form
   ___ C. it was almost April 15th

2. ___ A. the IRS, the state and Alice
   ___ B. the IRS, Alice's place of work, and Alice
   ___ C. the IRS, the state and the bank

3. ___ A. with her income tax return
   ___ B. find her 1040 form
   ___ C. get her W-2 form

4. ___ A. from her place of work
   ___ B. in the mail
   ___ C. from the bank

5. ___ A. an income tax return
   ___ B. a W-2 form
   ___ C. a 1040 form

148

Below is the story you just heard. Fill in the
blanks with the appropriate word.

It was almost April _____ and Alice needed some

_____ with her income tax _____. Mary agreed

to help _____. She was no expert _____ she

felt the short _____ was a snap. She _____ by

asking Alice for _____ W-2 form. When Alice _____

that the W-2 form _____ what she had gotten

_____ work, she gave Mary _____ three copies

of the _____. Mary explained that Alice _____

keep one copy of _____ W-2 form and should _____

one to the IRS _____ one to the state. _____

also said Alice needed the _____ form but Alice

didn't _____ getting it in the _____. Mary

assured her that _____ no problem because they

_____ get another form at _____ bank.

149

38

Alice Calls Long Distance

Look over the following sentences and make sure that you understand the words and the meaning of each sentence.

_____ A. "Oh, it's easy," Mary said reassuringly. "Just dial the area code and then dial 555-1212."

_____ B. "60%! Boy, that's a lot cheaper," Alice exclaimed. "Maybe I'll call my old classmate in Texas when you're finished."

_____ C. "It's eleven o'clock," Mary said to Alice. "I think I'll call my sister in California."

_____ D. "Because the rates go down 60% after eleven," Mary replied, picking up the receiver and dialing her sister's number.

_____ E. "Well, why don't you call information?" Mary advised.

_____ F. "No," Mary replied. "There's never any charge for calling information, even when it's long distance."

_____ G. "Here, you can do it now," Mary suggested. "My sister's line's busy."

_____ H. "Why do you always wait to call till after eleven p.m.?" Alice asked.

_____ I. "Isn't that another long distance call I'll be charged for?" Alice asked.

_____ J. Taking the receiver from Mary, Alice started to dial and then stopped.

_____ K. "How do I do that?" asked Alice, a little puzzled. "I always forget all those numbers."

_____ L. "Darn, I can't remember her number," she said.

Part II: Check the appropriate answer to each question
           after it is read to you.

1. ___ Yes, it is.   4. ___ Yes, she was.
    ___ Yes, there is.   ___ Yes, she does.
    ___ No, it isn't.   ___ No, Alice was.

2. ___ Yes, she was.   5. ___ Yes, there is.
    ___ Yes, it was.   ___ No, there isn't.
    ___ No, she wasn't.   ___ Yes, it is.

3. ___ No, she couldn't.
    ___ No, but Mary could.
    ___ Yes, she could.

Part III: Listen to the reading passage and then check the
           appropriate answer to each question.

1. ___ A. the rates were 60% cheaper
    ___ B. Mary always waited until after eleven to call
    ___ C. Mary was calling her sister in California

2. ___ A. call her sister in California
    ___ B. call her friend in Texas
    ___ C. call information

3. ___ A. the number for long distance information
    ___ B. her sister's telephone number
    ___ C. her friend's telephone number

4. ___ A. her sister's line was busy
    ___ B. calling information would be another long dis-
             tance call
    ___ C. she could get her friend's telephone number

5. ___ A. she had to call long distance after eleven p.m.
    ___ B. her sister lived in California
    ___ C. there was no charge for calling long distance
             information

152

Part IV: Below is the story you just heard. Fill in the blanks with the appropriate word.

Mary waited until after ___11 p.m.___ before calling her sister ___in___ California. Alice asked why ___she___ always waited until so ___late___ in the evening and ___Mary___ told her that the ___eve/night___ rates were 60% cheaper ___after___ eleven. When Alice heard ___this___, she decided to call ___her old___ friend in Texas. She ___took___ the receiver from Mary ___and___ started to dial, but ___when___ she realized that she ___didn't___ remember the phone number. ___M___ suggested she call information ___and___ gave Alice the correct ___number___ to dial. Alice wondered ___what___ she would be charged ___for___ the long distance call ___for___ information, but Mary assured ___her___ that there was never ___any___ charge for calling information, ___even when it's___ long distance.

153

CHAPTER
39

Alice Gets a Ticket for an Illegal Turn

Look over the following sentences and make sure
that you understand the words and the meaning of
each sentence.

_____ A. "What have I done, officer?" she asked, a little
frightened.

_____ B. "You mean I can't turn on a green light even when
there's no traffic coming from the other direction?"

_____ C. "Well, I'm afraid I've got to give you a ticket.
Let's see your license."

_____ D. Alice pulled over to the side of the street and
rolled down her window.

_____ E. "Sure, the light was green, but the arrow wasn't,"
he responded.

_____ F. "Pull over, lady," the policeman said to Alice as
he drove up beside her.

_____ G. "Twenty-five dollars is the usual fine for this kind
of a violation," he replied, writing up the ticket.

_____ H. "Not if there's a sign saying 'Turn on green arrow
only,'" the officer replied.

_____ I. "How much is this going to cost me?" Alice asked,
handing him her driver's license.

_____ J. "You made an illegal left turn at the last intersection, ma'am," he replied.

_____ K. "Oh, I didn't see that sign," Alice sighed.

_____ L. "Illegal?" Alice repeated. "But the light was
green!"

Check the appropriate answer to each question after it is read to you.

1. ___ No, she didn't.
   ___ Yes, she did.
   ___ No, she did.

2. ___ No, she didn't.
   ___ Yes, she did.
   ___ Yes, she didn't.

3. ___ Yes, it wasn't.
   ___ No, it wasn't.
   ___ Yes, it was.

4. ___ Yes, she did.
   ___ Yes, she didn't.
   ___ No, she didn't.

5. ___ No, it isn't.
   ___ No, it is.
   ___ Yes, it is.

Part III: Listen to the reading passage and then check the appropriate answer to each question.

1. ___ A. to pull out
   ___ B. to pull over
   ___ C. to turn left

2. ___ A. she didn't wait for the green arrow
   ___ B. she didn't wait for the green light
   ___ C. she turned on a red light

3. ___ A. about how much it was going to cost
   ___ B. about giving her license to the officer
   ___ C. about pulling over to the side of the road

4. ___ A. the light was red
   ___ B. the light was green
   ___ C. the green arrow was showing

5. ___ A. not seeing traffic coming from the other direction
   ___ B. an illegal left turn
   ___ C. turning on a green arrow

Below is the story you just heard. Fill in the
blanks with the appropriate word.

    Alice was frightened when _____ policeman

drove up beside _____ and told her to _____

over. When she learned _____ she had made an

_____ left turn she was _____. She had turned

left _____ the light was green _____ there

wasn't any traffic _____ from the other direction.

_____ Alice hadn't seen the _____--"Turn on

green arrow _____"--the officer had to _____

her a traffic ticket _____ making the illegal turn.

_____ Alice gave him her _____ license she

asked him _____ much the ticket would _____

her. While the officer _____ writing up the ticket,

_____ told her that the _____ fine for that

kind _____ violation was twenty-five dollars.

Alice Loses Her Wallet

Part I: Look over the following sentences and make sure
          that you understand the words and the meaning of
          each sentence.

____ A. "Well," Alice replied, after thinking for a minute,
          "I remember taking my wallet out of my purse to pay
          for my lunch."

____ B. "Well, I just came on duty," the lady responded,
          looking under the counter, "and I don't see it here.
          I'll go ask the manager."

____ C. "Do you have some change for the parking meter?"
          Mary asked Alice. "I just have bills."

____ D. "Well, we'll have to go back to the restaurant
          and see if it's there," Mary said, getting into her
          car.

____ E. "You're in luck, Miss Johnson," the cashier said,
          returning from the back room with her wallet. "The
          manager had put it back there for safekeeping."

____ F. "Do you remember putting it back in after paying
          your bill?" Mary prodded.

____ G. "I think so," Alice responded, opening her purse.
          "Oh, no! I can't find my wallet."

____ H. "Just try to calm down, Alice, and think when you
          last had it."

____ I. "Pardon me," Alice said to the cashier in the
          restaurant, "my name's Alice Johnson and I think I
          might have left my wallet here on the counter when
          I paid my bill."

____ J. "It's just not here. I can't find it anywhere in
          my purse," Alice answered. "Oh, what could I have
          done with it?"

____ K. "Yes--no--oh, I can't remember!" Alice sobbed.

____ L. "Oh, it's in there somewhere with all that junk,"
          Mary laughed. "Look again."

Part II: Check the appropriate answer to each question
after it is read to you.

1. ___ Yes, she did.
   ___ No, she didn't.
   ___ Yes, she was.

2. ___ Yes, she could.
   ___ No, Mary could.
   ___ No, she couldn't.

3. ___ Yes, she did.
   ___ Yes, she could.
   ___ No, she couldn't.

4. ___ Yes, they were.
   ___ No, they weren't.
   ___ Yes, they did.

5. ___ Yes, he had.
   ___ No, he hadn't.
   ___ No, he didn't.

Part III: Listen to the reading passage and then check the
answer to each question.

1. ___ A. she couldn't find her purse
   ___ B. she had paid her lunch bill
   ___ C. she couldn't find her wallet

2. ___ A. change for the parking meter
   ___ B. a lot of junk
   ___ C. her lost wallet

3. ___ A. because Alice wanted to pay her bill
   ___ B. because Alice might have left her wallet there
   ___ C. because the cashier had just come on duty

4. ___ A. in her purse
   ___ B. on the counter
   ___ C. in the back room

5. ___ A. for safekeeping
   ___ B. because a new cashier had come on duty
   ___ C. because the manager took it

160

Below is the story you just heard. Fill in the blanks with the appropriate word.

Mary asked Alice for _____ change for the parking

_____ but when Alice opened _____ purse, she

couldn't find _____ wallet. Mary was sure _____

was in her purse _____ with all the junk _____

had and told her _____ look again. Alice however

_____ find it anywhere in _____ purse so

Mary prodded _____ to think where she'd _____

had it. Alice remembered _____ it out of her

_____ to pay for her _____ but she couldn't

remember _____ it back after paying _____ bill.

Mary said they _____ have to go back _____ the

restaurant and see _____ it was there. When _____

got there Alice hurried _____ to the cashier and

_____ her that she thought _____ might have left

her _____ on the counter when _____ paid her bill.

The _____ had just come on _____ and she

couldn't see _____ under the counter so _____

went to the back room _____ ask the manager. When

_____ returned she had Alice's _____ with her.

The manager _____ put the wallet in _____ back room

for safekeeping.

CHAPTER
41

Alice Buys Gas

Look over the following sentences and make sure that you understand the words and the meaning of each sentence.

_____ A. In a moment he returned with a little gadget with a gauge which he used to draw some water out of the radiator.

_____ B. "Well," said Alice, "I guess that's it then--oh, I know, one more thing. Could you just quickly check the water in the battery?"

_____ C. "Sure thing, ma'am," replied the young man as he took the nozzle off the pump and put it in the gas tank.

_____ D. "Regular or lead-free?" the service station attendant asked Alice as she rolled down her window.

_____ E. "How about my antifreeze?" asked Alice, sticking her head out the window. "Can you check that too?"

_____ F. "Guess you're safe enough," he said. "The anti-freeze'll protect you until it gets below minus ten."

_____ G. Then, fixing the nozzle so it would shut off auto-matically, he walked to the front of the car and raised the hood.

_____ H. "Fill it up with lead-free," she said to him, "and would you mind checking the oil?"

_____ I. "Sure, it'll just take a second, but I'll have to get my antifreeze tester first," he said, hurrying into the station.

_____ J. "Your oil's okay, ma'am," he said, looking at Alice through the windshield.

_____ K. After studying the gauge for a minute he turned to Alice.

Check the appropriate answer to each question after it is read to you.

1. ___ Yes, she did.
   ___ No, she didn't.
   ___ Yes, she had.

2. ___ Yes, he did.
   ___ No, he didn't.
   ___ Yes, he had.

3. ___ Yes, it is.
   ___ No, it isn't.
   ___ Yes, it has.

4. ___ No, he didn't.
   ___ No, he hadn't.
   ___ Yes, he had.

5. ___ Yes, she did.
   ___ No, she didn't.
   ___ Yes, she was.

Part III: Listen to the reading passage and then check the appropriate answer to each question.

1. ___ A. the gas
   ___ B. the antifreeze
   ___ C. the oil

2. ___ A. in the back of the car
   ___ B. in the front of the car
   ___ C. under the hood

3. ___ A. to get the gas pump
   ___ B. to get the antifreeze
   ___ C. to get the antifreeze tester

4. ___ A. he pumped it out
   ___ B. he shut it off automatically
   ___ C. he drew it out

5. ___ A. check the oil
   ___ B. check the antifreeze
   ___ C. check the water in the battery

Below is the story you just heard. Fill in the
blanks with the appropriate word.

The attendant at the _____ station took the

nozzle _____ the lead-free pump _____ put it into

Alice's _____ tank. After he had _____ it to

shut off _____, he walked to the _____ of the

car and _____ the hood. First he _____ the

oil and then _____ got an antifreeze _____ from

inside the station _____ drew some water out

_____ the radiator. He studied _____ gauge

for a moment _____ then he told Alice _____ her

car was safe _____ it got below minus _____.

Alice thought for a _____ and then told him _____

was one more thing _____ needed done. She wanted

_____ water in the battery checked.

42

Alice Asks a Favor

Look over the following sentences and make sure that you understand the words and the meaning of each sentence.

____ A. "That's okay, Alice. Go ahead and tell me what it is."

____ B. "Oh, that's right. I forgot that you work today. Well, don't worry. You hurry up or you'll be late."

____ C. "A favor? Sure, Alice, just so it won't take more than a few minutes. I've got a class at nine."

____ D. "No, I don't want you to do that, Mark. You'll be late for class."

____ E. "Well, okay, Mark, if you really want to know. It's my car. It won't start."

____ F. "Hello, Mark. This is Alice. I hate to bother you but could I ask you a favor?"

____ G. "I won't be home later, Alice," Mark reminded her. "I go to work right after class."

____ H. "I'm already late, Alice! Another five minutes won't make any difference."

____ I. "No, Mark, I don't want you to be late for your class. I'll call back after it's over."

____ J. "For heaven's sake, Alice!" Mark insisted, a little annoyed. "Tell me what it is. Class or no class. Work or no work. Tell me what it is."

____ K. "Oh, is that it?" Mark sighed. "Well, I can't fix it this morning so I'll come by and drive you to work."

____ L. "Oh gee, I forgot you had a class," Alice apologized. "I shouldn't have called."

Check the appropriate answer to each question
after it is read to you.

1. ___ Yes, he did.
   ___ No, she called him.
   ___ Yes, he called her.

2. ___ Yes, she had.
   ___ No, he had.
   ___ Yes, she was.

3. ___ Yes, he was.
   ___ No, he wasn't.
   ___ No, he did.

4. ___ Yes, he did.
   ___ No, Alice did.
   ___ No, Alice was.

5. ___ Yes, she was.
   ___ Yes, she did.
   ___ No, Mark was.

Part III: Listen to the reading passage and then check the
appropriate answer to each question.

1. ___ A. to get a ride
   ___ B. to ask him a favor
   ___ C. to apologize for calling

2. ___ A. that Mark had a class
   ___ B. that her car wouldn't start
   ___ C. that she wanted a favor

3. ___ A. because he had a class at nine
   ___ B. because he had to go to work after class
   ___ C. because he couldn't fix her car then

4. ___ A. because she asked a favor
   ___ B. because Mark was going to be late
   ___ C. because her car wouldn't start

5. ___ A. fix her car
   ___ B. drive her to work
   ___ C. call her later

168

Below is the story you just heard. Fill in the
blanks with the appropriate word.

Alice called Mark to _____ him a favor. He

_____ happy to help as _____ as it wouldn't take

_____ more than a few _____ because he had a

_____ at nine. Alice had _____ about his class

and _____ for calling. She didn't _____ him to

be late _____ class so she said _____ call back

after it _____ over. But Mark reminded _____

that he had to _____ after his class and _____

be home later. When _____ heard this she told _____

not to worry. By _____ time Mark was a _____

annoyed and insisted that _____ tell him what she

_____. Alice then told him _____ she

needed help getting _____ car started. Since Mark

_____ fix it then he _____ he would come by

_____ drive her to work. _____ was already

late, so _____ five minutes wouldn't make _____

difference.

43

Alice Rides the City Bus

Look over the following sentences and make sure that you understand the words and the meaning of each sentence.

_____ A. "Not directly, miss," the number twenty bus driver answered. "When we reach MacArthur and Roosevelt you'll have to transfer."

_____ B. "Thank you," Alice said, putting the transfer slip in her purse. "How much will this be?"

_____ C. "Let's see, sixty cents," Alice said to herself as she dug into her purse. "Can you change a five?"

_____ D. After a few minutes the number twenty bus pulled up to the bus stop and the door opened.

_____ E. "No, ma'am," he answered. "You need to wait for a green number twenty bus."

_____ F. "It's easy, miss," the bus driver responded, handing Alice a slip of paper. "Just give this to the number twelve bus driver."

_____ G. "Oh dear," said Alice as she continued to search in her purse. "Twenty-five, thirty-five, forty-five, fifty, fifty-five--do you mind taking pennies?"

_____ H. "It should be along here in about 4 or 5 minutes," he added before he pulled away.

_____ I. "It's fifty cents plus ten cents for the transfer," the driver answered.

_____ J. "Will this bus take me to the East Grove Shopping Center?" Alice asked the driver at the bus stop.

_____ K. "No, miss," the bus driver answered. "I can't make change."

_____ L. "Transfer?" Alice repeated, a little puzzled. "How do I do that?"

_____ M. "I was told this bus'll take me to the East Grove Shopping Center," Alice said as she got on.

Check the appropriate answer to each question
after it is read to you.

1. ___ Yes, she was.   4. ___ Yes, they can.
   ___ No, she wasn't.   ___ Yes, they do.
   ___ Yes, it was.   ___ No, they can't.

2. ___ Yes, she would.   5. ___ Yes, she was.
   ___ No, she wouldn't.   ___ No, she wasn't.
   ___ No, they wouldn't.   ___ No, five dollars

3. ___ Yes, it did.
   ___ No, only ten cents.
   ___ No, sixty cents.

Listen to the reading passage and then check the
appropriate answer to each question.

1. ___ A. for the number twelve bus
   ___ B. for a bus to the East Grove Shopping Center
   ___ C. for a transfer slip

2. ___ A. to the bus stop
   ___ B. to the East Grove Shopping Center
   ___ C. to MacArthur and Roosevelt Streets

3. ___ A. give it to the number twelve bus driver
   ___ B. give it to the number twenty bus driver
   ___ C. put it in her purse

4. ___ A. he didn't have change
   ___ B. he couldn't make change
   ___ C. he didn't want change

5. ___ A. sixty cents
   ___ B. fifty cents
   ___ C. ten cents

172

Part IV: Below is the story you just heard. Fill in the
blanks with the appropriate word.

    Alice waited at the _____ stop for a bus _____
the East Grove Shopping _____. The first bus that
_____, however, wasn't the one _____ needed.
She had to _____ for a green number twenty _____.
When it came to _____ bus stop about five _____
later, Alice got on _____ asked the driver if _____
bus would take her _____ the shopping center. He
_____ Alice that she would _____ to transfer
to a _____ bus at MacArthur and _____ Streets.
When Alice asked _____ she would transfer, the
_____ driver gave her a _____ slip and told
her _____ give it to the _____ of the number
twelve. He _____ told Alice the ride _____ cost
sixty cents--fifty cents for _____ first bus and ten
cents _____ the transfer. Alice asked _____ if
he could change _____ five-dollar bill, but _____
answered that he couldn't _____ change. Alice then
dug _____ her purse and found _____--some of
it in _____.

173

44

Alice Asks For Information
in the Library

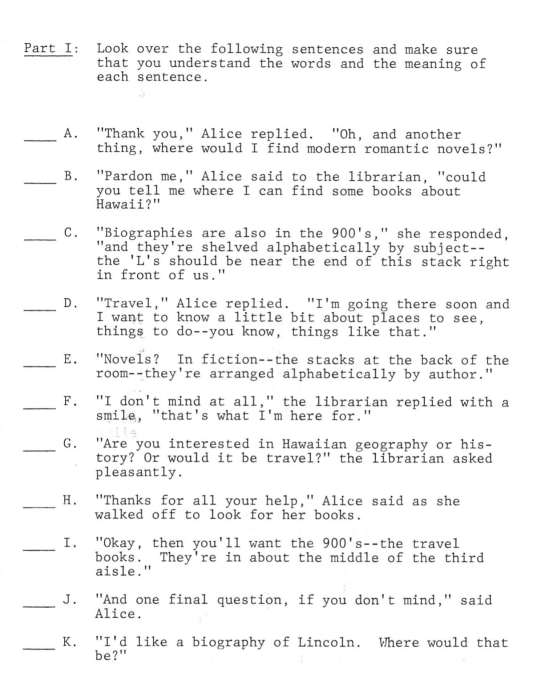

Part I: Look over the following sentences and make sure
that you understand the words and the meaning of
each sentence.

____ A. "Thank you," Alice replied. "Oh, and another
thing, where would I find modern romantic novels?"

____ B. "Pardon me," Alice said to the librarian, "could
you tell me where I can find some books about
Hawaii?"

____ C. "Biographies are also in the 900's," she responded,
"and they're shelved alphabetically by subject--
the 'L's should be near the end of this stack right
in front of us."

____ D. "Travel," Alice replied. "I'm going there soon and
I want to know a little bit about places to see,
things to do--you know, things like that."

____ E. "Novels? In fiction--the stacks at the back of the
room--they're arranged alphabetically by author."

____ F. "I don't mind at all," the librarian replied with a
smile, "that's what I'm here for."

____ G. "Are you interested in Hawaiian geography or history? Or would it be travel?" the librarian asked
pleasantly.

____ H. "Thanks for all your help," Alice said as she
walked off to look for her books.

____ I. "Okay, then you'll want the 900's--the travel
books. They're in about the middle of the third
aisle."

____ J. "And one final question, if you don't mind," said
Alice.

____ K. "I'd like a biography of Lincoln. Where would that
be?"

175

Part II: Check the appropriate answer to each question after it is read to you.

1. ___ Yes, she was.
   ___ No, she wasn't.
   ___ Yes, that's right.

4. ___ Yes, she did.
   ___ No, she didn't.
   ___ No, a geography.

2. ___ Yes, she was.
   ___ No, she wasn't.
   ___ Yes, she did.

5. ___ Yes, they are.
   ___ No, by subject.
   ___ Yes, they were.

3. ___ Yes, it is.
   ___ No, it isn't.
   ___ No, by subject.

Part III: Listen to the reading passage and then check the appropriate answer to each question.

1. ___ A. to find some books about Hawaii
   ___ B. to find the 900's
   ___ C. to read a novel about Lincoln

2. ___ A. she wanted to read about geography
   ___ B. she wanted to read modern romantic novels
   ___ C. she was going there soon

3. ___ A. in the 900's
   ___ B. alphabetically by author
   ___ C. alphabetically by subject

4. ___ A. alphabetically by subject
   ___ B. alphabetically by author
   ___ C. like the romantic novels

5. ___ A. arranged the novels alphabetically
   ___ B. read about Hawaii
   ___ C. thanked the librarian

176

Part IV: Below is the story you just heard. Fill in the
          blanks with the appropriate word.

Alice wanted to find _____ library books about

Hawaii _____ she asked the librarian _____ help.

The librarian wanted _____ know if Alice was _____

in Hawaiian geography, history _____ travel. Since

Alice was _____ there soon, she wanted _____ travel

book. The librarian _____ her that the travel _____

were in the 900's. _____ also wanted to find _____

romantic novels, which the _____ said were arranged

alphabetically _____ author. To find a _____

of Lincoln, which Alice _____ wanted, the librarian

told _____ to look in the _____. These books

were shelved _____ by subject. After hearing

_____ Alice thanked the librarian _____ went off

to look _____ her books.

Alice Decides
to Make a Budget

Part I: Look over the following sentences and make sure that you understand the words and the meaning of each sentence.

_____ A. "Because I'm always broke!" Alice sighed. "And I thought maybe a budget would help me economize."

_____ B. "Good idea, Alice," Mark answered. "If you'd stop charging things it would be easier to save money."

_____ C. "Well, Alice," answered Mark with a laugh, "just remember. Essentials are boring yet necessary, but luxuries are fun!"

_____ D. "A budget? What do you want a budget for?" Mark asked, a little surprised.

_____ E. "And you're sure you've got the willpower?" Mark teased. "It'd mean you'd have to give up buying things on credit, you know."

_____ F. "And another thing," Mark continued, "you'll have to start buying only essentials and cut out luxuries."

_____ G. "Oh, I think I could stick to it," Alice replied. "It just takes a little willpower."

_____ H. "Ah, there's the problem, Mark," Alice sighed. "It's so hard for me to draw a line between essentials and luxuries."

_____ I. "Sure, I know that," Alice said. "So I'll have to put away all my credit cards so I won't be tempted."

_____ J. "It could really help you economize," Mark agreed, "but only if you stick to it."

_____ K. "Mark, would you help me make a budget?" Alice pleaded.

Check the appropriate answer to each question
after it is read to you.

1. ___ Yes, he did.
   ___ No, Alice was.
   ___ No, Alice did.

2. ___ Yes, she did.
   ___ Yes, she was.
   ___ No, Mark did.

3. ___ Yes, she would.
   ___ Yes, she did.
   ___ Yes, it would.

4. ___ Yes, she did.
   ___ Yes, she would.
   ___ No, Mark would.

5. ___ Yes, he did.
   ___ No, boring.
   ___ No, he wouldn't.

Part III: Listen to the reading passage and then check the
appropriate answer to each question.

1. ___ A. because she had enough willpower.
   ___ B. because she was always broke
   ___ C. because she charged things

2. ___ A. by buying luxuries
   ___ B. with a little willpower
   ___ C. if Mark helped her to make it

3. ___ A. because she was not going to buy luxuries
   ___ B. so she wouldn't be tempted
   ___ C. because Mark thought it was a good idea

4. ___ A. both essentials and luxuries
   ___ B. luxuries but not essentials
   ___ C. essentials but not luxuries

5. ___ A. they were fun yet necessary
   ___ B. they were boring yet fun
   ___ C. they were boring yet necessary

Part IV: Below is the story you just read. Fill in the blanks with the appropriate word.

Alice wanted Mark to _____ her make a budget _____ she was always broke. _____ thought that maybe a _____ would help her economize. _____ agreed that it could _____ her but only if _____ stuck to it. Alice _____ that with a little _____, she could stick to _____ budget without any problem. _____ teased Alice about having _____ willpower, adding that _____ would have to give _____ buying things on credit. _____ said she'd put away _____ credit cards so she _____ be tempted, which Mark _____ was a good idea. _____ thing she'd have to _____ was start buying only _____ and cut out luxuries. _____ Alice this was a _____ because it was hard _____ her to draw a _____ between essentials and luxuries. _____ laughingly told her to _____ that essentials were boring _____ necessary, while luxuries were fun.

181

Alice is Late for Dinner

Look over the following sentences and make sure that you understand the words and the meaning of each sentence.

_____ A. "Should I tell them all my reasons for being so late?" Alice asked, reaching for the phone.

_____ B. "5:30 already," Alice repeated. "Oh no, I really am late."

_____ C. "What am I going to say?" Alice sighed. "I'm afraid I've ruined their dinner party."

_____ D. "What time is it?" Alice asked Mary as she rushed into the room. "I'm running late today."

_____ E. "No, not over the phone," Mary advised. "You can tell them all that once you're there."

_____ F. "Yes, I was," Alice cried, "but I forgot my purse and had to run back for it, the bus was late, then I. . . "

_____ G. "5:30," Mary answered, glancing at the clock.

_____ H. "Just explain that you're very sorry but you're going to be late," Mary responded.

_____ I. "Weren't you supposed to be at your boss's for dinner by now?" Mary asked.

_____ J. "Well, you shouldn't be standing here telling me all this," Mary interrupted. "You'd better phone them so they won't wait dinner for you."

_____ K. "And what's more important," she added, "be sure and tell them to go ahead and eat without you."

Part II: Check the appropriate answer to each question
           after it is read to you.

1. ___ Yes, she was.   4. ___ Yes, she was.
   ___ No, she wasn't.   ___ No, she wasn't.
   ___ Yes, she did.   ___ Yes, she did.

2. ___ Yes, she was.   5. ___ Yes, she did.
   ___ No, she wasn't.   ___ No, not over the
   ___ Yes, it was.   phone.
                                 ___ Yes, over the phone.

3. ___ Yes, they were.
   ___ No, they weren't.
   ___ Yes, she was.

Part III: Listen to the reading passage and then check the
            appropriate answer to each question.

1. ___ A. be at her boss's for dinner at 5:30
   ___ B. be late for the bus
   ___ C. be late for dinner at her boss's

2. ___ A. that she would be late for dinner
   ___ B. why she was running so late
   ___ C. that she had to call her boss

3. ___ A. that she was late for dinner
   ___ B. that she go ahead and eat
   ___ C. that she call and let them know she would be late

4. ___ A. Alice was late for dinner
   ___ B. they go ahead and eat without Alice
   ___ C. Alice was invited to her boss's for dinner

5. ___ A. give them her reasons for being late
   ___ B. ruin their dinner party
   ___ C. go back for her purse

184

Part IV: Below is the story you just heard. Fill in the
          blanks with the appropriate word.

      Alice was surprised when _____ rushed into the

room _____ Mary told her it _____ 5:30. She was

supposed _____ be at her boss's _____ dinner by

then and _____ upset to realize that _____ was

late. She started _____ tell Mary why she _____

running so late but _____ interrupted her and

suggested _____ call and let them _____ she

would be late. _____ thought it was very _____

that Alice tell them _____ go ahead and eat _____

her. Alice wondered if _____ should tell all her

_____ for being so late _____ the phone.

Mary, however, _____ her to wait until _____

got there.

CHAPTER
47

Alice Loses a Library Book

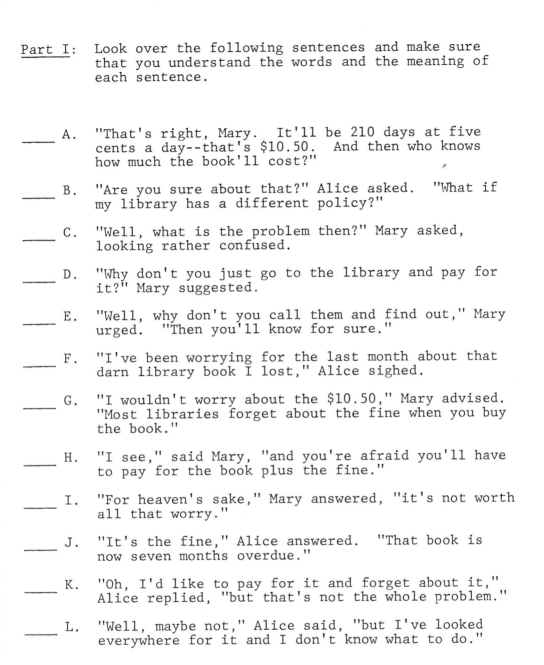

Part I: Look over the following sentences and make sure that you understand the words and the meaning of each sentence.

_____ A. "That's right, Mary. It'll be 210 days at five cents a day--that's $10.50. And then who knows how much the book'll cost?"

_____ B. "Are you sure about that?" Alice asked. "What if my library has a different policy?"

_____ C. "Well, what is the problem then?" Mary asked, looking rather confused.

_____ D. "Why don't you just go to the library and pay for it?" Mary suggested.

_____ E. "Well, why don't you call them and find out," Mary urged. "Then you'll know for sure."

_____ F. "I've been worrying for the last month about that darn library book I lost," Alice sighed.

_____ G. "I wouldn't worry about the $10.50," Mary advised. "Most libraries forget about the fine when you buy the book."

_____ H. "I see," said Mary, "and you're afraid you'll have to pay for the book plus the fine."

_____ I. "For heaven's sake," Mary answered, "it's not worth all that worry."

_____ J. "It's the fine," Alice answered. "That book is now seven months overdue."

_____ K. "Oh, I'd like to pay for it and forget about it," Alice replied, "but that's not the whole problem."

_____ L. "Well, maybe not," Alice said, "but I've looked everywhere for it and I don't know what to do."

187

Part II: Check the appropriate answer to each question after it is read to you.

1. ___ Yes, she had.
   ___ Yes, she was.
   ___ No, she wasn't.

4. ___ Yes, she did.
   ___ Yes, $10.50
   ___ No, she didn't.

2. ___ Yes, it was.
   ___ Yes, she was.
   ___ No, seven months.

5. ___ Yes, she did.
   ___ Yes, she was.
   ___ No, Mary urged Alice.

3. ___ Yes, she was.
   ___ Yes, she did.
   ___ No, only for the book.

Part III: Listen to the reading passage and then check the appropriate answer to each question.

1. ___ A. calling the library
   ___ B. that her library might have a different policy
   ___ C. a library book she had lost

2. ___ A. because it wasn't worth a lot of worry
   ___ B. because she had lost the book
   ___ C. because she was afraid she would have to pay for the book plus the fine

3. ___ A. seven weeks at five cents a day
   ___ B. five cents a month for seven months
   ___ C. five cents a day for 210 days

4. ___ A. because most libraries forget about the fine when the book is paid for
   ___ B. because the book would be $10.50
   ___ C. because she was going to call the library

5. ___ A. to tell them about the lost book
   ___ B. to find out about their lost book policy
   ___ C. to pay the fine

Below is the story you just heard. Fill in the
         blanks with the appropriate word.

        Alice had been worrying _____ a library book she

_____ lost. Mary told her _____ wasn't worth

a lot _____ worry, but Alice had _____ everywhere

for it and _____ didn't know what to _____ .

Mary suggested that Alice _____ to the library and

_____ for the book. Alice _____ have liked

to pay _____ it and forget about _____ but she

was worried _____ would also have to _____ a

fine. Since the _____ was seven months overdue,

_____ knew the fine would _____ five cents

a day _____ 210 days which would _____ $10.50.

Mary advised her _____ to worry about the _____

since most libraries forget _____ fine when the

_____ is paid for. Alice _____ her library

might have _____ different policy so Mary _____

her to call and _____ out for sure.

Alice Has To
Refuse an Invitation

Look over the following sentences and make sure that you understand the words and the meaning of each sentence.

____ A. "Well, at least you can advise me whether to write or call," Alice said. "I'm not sure which is better."

____ B. "Don't worry about making a mistake," Mary advised. "Just be polite and truthful."

____ C. "Very, very carefully," Mary laughed.

____ D. "Sure, if your reason for not going will help her to understand your refusal," Mary answered.

____ E. "I'm not so sure I can help," Mary responded more seriously. "Refusing an invitation can be pretty tricky."

____ F. "Say, Mary, if you were me, how would you refuse a party invitation from your boss's wife?" Alice asked.

____ G. "I guess you're right, Mary," Alice said thought-fully. "I really am sorry I can't go to her party so I guess I should be sure to let her know that."

____ H. "Gosh, I don't know, Alice. I guess a written refusal is better if it's done right."

____ I. "Should I tell her why I can't go?" asked Alice as she began to write.

____ J. "That's just it," Alice exclaimed. "I've got to do it right and I'm afraid I'll make a mistake."

____ K. "That's the idea," Mary exclaimed. "Write how much you appreciated receiving the invitation and that you regret very much not being able to attend."

____ L. "Oh come on, Mary," Alice pleaded, "this is serious. I need help."

Check the appropriate answer to each question
after it is read to you.

1. ___ No, she wasn't.   4. ___ No, she wasn't.
   ___ Yes, she was.   ___ No, Mary was.
   ___ Alice was sure.   ___ Yes, she was.

2. ___ No, she didn't.   5. ___ Yes, she was.
   ___ No, Alice did.   ___ No, she wasn't.
   ___ Yes, she did.   ___ No, Mary was.

3. ___ Yes, she did.
   ___ No, she didn't.
   ___ No, Alice didn't.

Part III: Listen to the reading passage and check the
appropriate answer to each question.

1. ___ A. avoid going to a party with her boss's wife
   ___ B. invite her boss's wife to a party
   ___ C. refuse a party invitation from her boss's wife

2. ___ A. to write the refusal
   ___ B. to make a mistake
   ___ C. to be very, very careful

3. ___ A. pretty tricky
   ___ B. polite and truthful
   ___ C. without mistakes

4. ___ A. she was sorry that she couldn't go to the party
   ___ B. she didn't have a reason for not going to the
          party
   ___ C. she didn't think she would make a mistake

5. ___ A. she needed Mary's advice
   ___ B. she appreciated receiving the invitation
   ___ C. she was afraid she wouldn't refuse it correctly

Part IV: Below is the story you just heard. Fill in the blanks with the appropriate word.

Alice didn't know how _____ refuse a party invitation _____ her boss's wife so _____ asked Mary's advice. She _____ to know if it _____ better to write or _____ to say she couldn't _____ . Mary thought that a _____ refusal was better if _____ was done right. But _____ was the problem, Alice confessed. _____ was afraid she wouldn't _____ it right and would _____ a mistake. Mary tried _____ reassure her and told _____ not to worry. All _____ needed to do was _____ a polite and truthful response. _____ was convinced that that _____ good advice because she _____ really sorry that she _____ go to the party _____ she had truly appreciated _____ the invitation. As she _____ to write, she asked _____ if she should include _____ reason why she couldn't _____ . Mary thought she should_____ it would help her _____ wife understand better.

Alice Doesn't Buy
a Thank-You Gift

Part I: Look over the following sentences and make sure that you understand the words and the meaning of each sentence.

_____ A.   "You mean you're going to give her a gift just for having you over for dinner?" Mark asked, a little surprised.

_____ B.   "A thank-you note?" Alice repeated. "Do you really think that would be enough?"

_____ C.   "They don't? Well, what do they do then?" Alice asked.

_____ D.   "Sorry, Mark, it's not for you," Alice laughed. "It's a thank-you gift."

_____ E.   "Say, Mark, I've got to buy a gift. Want to come with me?" Alice asked.

_____ F.   "Sure, what's wrong with that?" Alice replied. "I want to show my thanks."

_____ G.   "Why sure, Alice," Mark answered. "A thank-you note'll do the trick."

_____ H.   "That's right. It's for my boss's wife," said Alice, still smiling. "She had me over for dinner last night."

_____ I.   "Oh, today most people just call or mention their thanks in person when they get a chance."

_____ J.   "A gift?" Mark smiled. "How did you know my birthday was coming up?"

_____ K.   "In fact," he added, "nowadays most people don't even send a thank-you note."

_____ L.   "Well, you could show your thanks with a thank-you note," Mark suggested.

_____ M.   "Oh, I see," sighed Mark in mock disappointment, "it's for somebody else."

Part II: Check the appropriate answer to each question
after it is read to you.

1. ___ Yes, she was.   4. ___ Yes, he did.
   ___ No, she wasn't.   ___ No, he didn't.
   ___ No, he wasn't.   ___ No, Alice did.

2. ___ Yes, he was.   5. ___ No, never.
   ___ No, he wasn't.   ___ No, they don't.
   ___ Yes, she was.   ___ Yes, they do.

3. ___ Yes, he did.
   ___ No, with a note.
   ___ Yes, she did.

Part III: Listen to the reading passage and then check the
appropriate answer to each question.

1. ___ A. buy a thank-you gift
   ___ B. send a thank-you note
   ___ C. mention her thanks in person

2. ___ A. because most people today don't even send a
          thank-you note
   ___ B. because her boss's wife had had her over for
          dinner
   ___ C. because Mark wanted her to

3. ___ A. that Alice had had dinner at her boss's house
   ___ B. that Alice thought a thank-you note would do the
          trick
   ___ C. that Alice was planning to buy a thank-you gift
          just for going to dinner

4. ___ A. by buying thank-you gifts
   ___ B. by sending thank-you notes
   ___ C. by calling or mentioning their thanks in person

5. ___ A. eaten dinner at her boss's house
   ___ B. bought a thank-you gift for her boss's wife
   ___ C. mentioned her thanks in person

196

Part IV: Below is the story you just heard. Fill in the blanks with the appropriate word.

Alice asked Mark to _____ with her to look

_____ a thank-you gift. _____ thought she

needed a _____ because her boss's wife _____

had her over for _____ the night before. Mark

_____ surprised that Alice was _____ to buy

a gift _____ for going to dinner. _____ didn't

know how else _____ show her thanks but _____

was sure that a _____ note would do the _____.

He told her that _____ fact most people nowadays

_____ not even send a _____ note. Alice was

surprised _____ hear that and asked _____

people did. Calling on _____ telephone or mentioning

it _____ person, Mark explained, are _____

people today show their _____.

197

50

Alice Asks For Help to Fix Her Leaky Faucet

Look over the following sentences and make sure that you understand the words and the meaning of each sentence.

_____ A. "What are you looking for under there?" asked Alice, a little puzzled.

_____ B. "Take the faucet apart?" Alice repeated. "Why do you have to do that?"

_____ C. As Mary followed Alice into the bathroom, she noticed that the faucet was dripping a lot.

_____ D. "Oh, my last bill was awful," Alice responded. "That's why I want to get this fixed."

_____ E. "Mary, could you show me how to fix a leaky faucet?" Alice asked.

_____ F. "Shut-off valves? You mean we have to shut off the water to fix the faucet?"

_____ G. "You're wasting a lot of water with that drip," she observed. "Your water bill must be awfully high."

_____ H. "It's the cold water faucet in my bathroom sink," Alice answered. "Come on, I'll show you."

_____ I. "I wanted to see if you had any shut-off valves under your basin," Mary replied, "but I'm afraid you don't."

_____ J. "Well, I'll have to put in a new washer and I can't do that unless I take the faucet apart."

_____ K. "That's right, Alice. We'll have to shut off the water before I take the faucet apart."

_____ L. "Well, let me see," said Mary, looking under the wash basin.

_____ M. "Sure, I've fixed lots of them," Mary replied. "Which one is it?"

<u>Part II</u>: Check the appropriate answer to each question
after it is read to you.

1. ___ Yes, she did.   4. ___ Yes, it was.
   ___ No, she didn't.   ___ No, it wasn't.
   ___ Yes, she didn't.   ___ Yes, it wasn't.

2. ___ Yes, she did.   5. ___ Yes, she had.
   ___ No, she didn't.   ___ No, she hadn't.
   ___ Yes, she didn't.   ___ Yes, she hadn't.

3. ___ Yes, she could.
   ___ No, she couldn't.
   ___ Yes, she couldn't.

<u>Part III</u>: Listen to the reading passage and then check the
appropriate answer to each question.

1. ___ A. why she was wasting water
   ___ B. which faucet was dripping
   ___ C. how to fix a leaky faucet

2. ___ A. Alice's bathroom sink
   ___ B. Alice's kitchen sink
   ___ C. Alice's shut-off valve

3. ___ A. she didn't have any shut-off valves
   ___ B. she was wasting a lot of water
   ___ C. she needed a new washer

4. ___ A. that the faucet was dripping a lot
   ___ B. that Alice didn't have any shut-off valves
   ___ C. that Alice's last water bill had been awfully high

5. ___ A. take the faucet apart
   ___ B. take the valve apart
   ___ C. take the basin apart

Below is the story you just heard. Fill in the
blanks with the appropriate word.

Alice asked Mary to _____ her fix a leaky

_____ water faucet in her _____ sink. As soon

as _____ walked into the bathroom _____ fix it,

she saw _____ the faucet was dripping _____ lot.

She knew that _____ leaky faucet could waste

_____ lot of water and _____ said that Alice's

water _____ must really be awfully _____.

Alice agreed that her _____ bill had been awful

_____ that was why she _____ to get the leak

_____. Mary looked under the _____ basin to

see if _____ had shut-off valves _____ there

weren't any there. _____ had not realized that

_____ would have to shut _____ the water

to fix _____ faucet. Mary explained to _____

that she was going _____ have to put in _____

new washer to stop _____ drip. She couldn't do

_____ until she had shut _____ the water

and taken _____ faucet apart.

201

INDEX